How to Stock a Home Library Inexpensively

Third Edition

by Jane A. Williams

Published by

Bluestocking Press
P.O. Box 1014
Dept. 3H
Placerville, CA 95667-1014
1-800-959-8586

How to Stock a Home Library Inexpensively, third edition

Copyright © 1995 by Jane A. Williams
Published by Bluestocking Press

Cover Design by Bob O'Hara, Georgetown, CA

Printed in the United States of America.

Library of Congress Cataloging-in-Publication Data
Williams, Jane A., 1950-
    How to stock a home library inexpensively / Jane A. Williams. -- 3rd ed.
        p.   cm.
    Rev. ed. of: How to stock a quality home library inexpensively. c1989.
    Includes bibliographical references and index.
    ISBN 0-942617-18-5   (alk. paper)
    1. Book collecting.   2. Books--Purchasing.   3. Private libraries.
    I. How to stock a quality home library inexpensively.   II. Title.
    Z987.W486   1995
    027'.1--dc20   95-15945
                                                        CIP

Published by:
Bluestocking Press
P.O. Box 1014
Dept. 3H
Placerville, CA 95667-1014
1-800-959-8586

Contents

"It is a great thing
to start life
with a small number of
really good books

which are your very own."

Sir Arthur Conan Doyle
THROUGH THE MAGIC DOOR, 1908

1

Books and Budgets

Stocking a home library can be very expensive. Trade paperback books today average[1] $18.00, hardcover books average $31.00, and mass market paperbacks average $5.00. Most budgets won't stretch to buy a substantial home library at these prices.

By following the suggestions in this book, however, you can reduce the cost of manyy of the books and other resources you buy for your home library. For example, instead of paying $18 for a softcover book, you may pay one dollar or less. Instead of paying $1729 for a set of THE GREAT BOOKS OF THE WESTERN WORLD, you may be able to purchase a set for less than $200. There are even ways to stock a substantial home library by subsidizing its cost from other areas of the household budget.

But why have a home library? What are its benefits? Without benefits, ten cents is too much to spend towards stocking a good home library. Why not borrow from your local library and avoid the expense of a private book collection entirely?

[1] Reported in Publishers Weekley, January 24, 1994. The figures reflect R.R. Bowker's 1992 average per-volume prices.

2

Benefits of a Home Library

Children and the Home Library

Books in the home provide children with extraordinary benefits. They have immediate access to good literature, resource materials, vocabulary sources, reference information, pictures, photographs and more. All this helps turn nonreaders into readers and readers into writers. Let me explain.

In my home our house is, and always has been, cluttered with books. No room of the house is exempt from our ever-expanding library. I've tried to donate some books to make room for newcomers but this isn't an easy task. It's like turning out a dear friend. And some member of the family always seems to find each potential discard as their personal favorite. I feel as though I'm giving away memories.

Having books around invites browsing, participation, reading, and playing. In my home children use books to play library, book store, or school. Books become houses and boats for dolls, roads for cars, flower presses, and clipboards for writing stories. They bind these stories to make their own books. For them the transition from reader to writer has been a natural process.

The activity of play often leads to the enjoyment of reading as a part of their "road" catches a driver's attention, who then pulls off the "road" to read.

Children learn by example. When parents read books from their home library, their prereading children wonder what is so important on the pages of those books. How can all those words be more interesting to Mom or Dad than the mudpies they are baking? Children want to discover for themselves what you find so fascinating about books. At one or two years of age they can't read a word, but they'll pretend to read because they see their Mom and Dad reading. From this desire to do what Mom and Dad and older siblings do, stems their first motivation to learn to read.

Little children enjoy having the same story read and reread. Without their own home library, they won't be able to grab their favorite book night after night. You might see this as a disadvantage if you've just read THE LITTLE RED HEN for the thirtieth time. It won't seem quite so tedious, however, if you realize that reading THE LITTLE RED HEN *again* is fostering a love of reading in your child. He is also very likely beginning his first efforts towards reading himself.

Through repetitive read-aloud children often memorize stories, and before long you'll probably see your child snuggled in a chair reading that same story, word for exact word, to her favorite doll or stuffed animal. Your child is probably reading from memory, and

she'll ask you questions about the letters and words on the page, in her effort to understand those words and letters. Before long she'll make the connection between the sounds of the letters and the written word on the page.

This can't happen as easily if children don't have ready access to books. Be sure to place children's books in areas of your home where little arms can reach them without the aid of an adult or older sibling.

Besides buying the colorful cardboard books designed for toddlers, you might also consider buying a few books with paper pages. If other family members read books with paper pages your toddler will eventually want similar material for himself. Buy a couple of books at a garage sale for a dime — books you really wouldn't want for your personal library — then if they are destroyed by the curious fingers of an exploring youngster you won't be focused on the damage done to a book you love — but on teaching the toddler how to handle books. Keep these books in reserve. When your toddler first insists on having a book like Mom's or Dad's, make these available to him and use them to teach your child how to care for books — no tearing, chewing, or sharing with the dog. We want to encourage use — not abuse.

When parents spend time reading to children and sharing picture books with them, their children are more likely to associate the calm, quiet, loving times spent snuggled by Mom or Dad with the pleasures of a good story. This can contribute to life-long habits of relaxation through reading rather than television.

Books offer an alternative to television. If books are readily available at home it makes it much easier to reach for the bookcase rather than the remote control.

Because we share so many stories during read-aloud, book's characters and themes provide great fodder for discussions. Many times I use a character or incident in a story to help explain something that's happening in the real world today.

Children are naturally curious and their minds full of questions. They learn best when they have a need to know something. A good home reference library can facilitate the independent learning process because it equips a child with the tools necessary to research subjects in which he is interested — at the time he is interested. It places control of the learning process in the hands of the child.

Unfortunately, young children's interests are very often fleeting. When they want to know something, they want to know it at that very moment. If they have to wait for a trip to the public library to find their answers they'll often move on to other interests and other questions. With the home library, however, you do have a distinct learning advantage over families without such a resource at their disposal. The opportunities to capitalize on spontaneous learning situations are more frequent since the reference material is handy.

The home library can be a catalyst to further research. If your children exhaust the resources in their own home library, encourage them to conduct further research at their school and public libraries.

Moods change. The book I read last night might not be the one that interests me tonight. Children are no different. The book that seemed so interesting at the public library may appear boring at bedtime. Some nights a child wants fiction, other nights nonfiction. Once in a while she wants fantasy, other times comedy, or maybe even mystery. We can't predict our children's moods any better than they can — any better than we can predict our own. By having a varied large home library we can always find something to suit both our children's and our own interests. We are always prepared.

Consider budgeting monthly for books as you do for groceries, utilities, taxes, housing, and insurance. By doing so, your children will realize that in your home, books — like budgets — have a high priority. In your home, books are possessions worth owning. In your home, books are possessions you plan for. In your home, books represent literacy, knowledge and education. In your home literacy, knowledge and education are considered essential to your children's intellectual and financial future.

Adults and Home Libraries

Having a good adult reference library is a time-saver and a mind saver. For example, the household cook usually has a shelf of cook-books. Many family's have members who have special dietary restrictions. Their cook-book shelves might include books on nutrition, vitamins, and specialty cookbooks. If they had to visit the public library every time they needed to verify nutrition information they'd be using up valuable time and gasoline. In addition, many public libraries have had their funds cut, so patrons are finding it more and more difficult to find what they need locally. Interlibrary loan is usually available but this sometimes involves a fee as well as time to ship the book to the requesting branch.

Sometimes my life is so busy I haven't the time to read a book in the two to three-week period allotted by the library. I find it discon-certing to feel pressured into reading quickly that which I reserve for relaxation and enjoy-ment. With a home library I can take all the time I need to read a book.

My family's "how to" and self-help books have saved us bundles of money. These books, which are as necessary and useful to us as a dictionary is to most people, include: car maintenance manuals, health books, financial planning books, reading and educational re-source guides, marketing books, construction handbooks, and the list goes on.

When I look on my library shelves and see specific book titles, I remember the pleasure I had reading those books whether for entertain-ment or self-education. I recall the special moments I shared with my children while read-ing a particular story, or the discoveries we made together when we raced to the encyclo-pedias to find out what skunks eat.

If these benefits make sense for your family the next concern is affordability.

3

Benefits vs. Cost
of the Home Library

Having identified several benefits of owning a good home library — the big problem in most households, including my own, is how to afford such a library.

One way to curtail the cost of a home library is to identify your family's needs. Avoid buying books, no matter how cheaply you can acquire them, if they don't meet the current or future needs of a member of your family. So the first thing to do before you begin to purchase books, is to decide which books you want to place on those library shelves.

4

Essential Items for Your Home Library

Books and Beyond

When we think of libraries, we think of books. But this is no longer the case. Nowadays, many public libraries stock CDs, audio-cassettes, books on tape, videos, and computers with access to the internet. Your home library needn't be any different.

Reference Materials

It is important to have a multi-level reference library available for your family. If each member of the family is at a different reading level and has different interests, each will need reference books that are appropriate for their individual ages and interests. For example, if you have a five-year old and a thirteen year-old, in addition to the adults in a household, you might have a set of CHILDREN'S BRITANNICA, for ages 7-14, (20 volume set currently sells for $329.49), and a set of WORLD BOOK or BRITANNICA ENCYCLOPEDIA. Depending on other interests — a science encyclopedia, art reference books or encyclopedia of animals may be apropos. This can get expensive, but there are ways to purchase some of these books inexpensively, which I'll explain later.

Reference materials essential to any home library include: a current atlas and globe, an up-to-date timetable or timeline, encyclopedia (either books or on CD Rom), an unabridged dictionary and a thesaurus, an almanac, a first aid book, nutrition book, if religious — the family's holy book, the Franklin Digital Book® System and a computer. Other possibilities might include: special interest encyclopedias (i.e., science, animals), parenting books, craft and cook books, financial planning and investment guides, philosophy, history, geography, economics books, religious training, and auto repair manuals, to name a few. The possibilities are endless.

The Franklin Digital Book® System is a hand-held portable reference source. A computer is wonderful, but you've heard the expression, the right tool for the right job. A computer is stationery, and you need to go to it when you need information. Portable laptop computers are available, but these are not as convenient as the Franklin Digital Book® System that is held in one hand and is slightly larger than a small hand-held calculator. It doesn't have the memory of a portable lap top computer, but it is small enough to slip in a pocket, purse or fanny pack. It has various digital books that pop into its chambers: a dictionary, the Concise Columbia Encyclopedia, and others. I use the dictionary and encyclopedia the most, especially on research trips. It helps to have such a handy source of data when visiting historical sites. For example, in Boston, one might wonder exactly what years did Paul Revere live? Where exactly was John Adam's home? As questions come to mind, answers are only a keypunch away. Children can use it as a spell checker for writing, for additional background information as they read books, as a vocabulary builder to help them understand unfamiliar words. I highly suspect most children wouldn't take the time to leaf through the pages of a dictionary. Nor would they want to leave the cozy corner where they're reading to boot up their tabletop com-

puter. Engrossed in a novel, however, they are likely to reach for their digital book system and punch in a word to secure more information. It's quick and won't detract from the momentum of the story.

Regarding timetables, I like the TIMETABLES OF HISTORY™ published by Simon & Schuster, which is a book, not a wall chart. With this book you can make your own timeline with butcher paper. As you read books, fiction or nonfiction, chart on a blank piece of paper the time period in which the book takes place. Use your TIMETABLES OF HISTORY to discover what else was happening in the world at that time. Place your family's ancestral history on this developing timeline as well (immediate family, grandparents, great grandparents, etc.) so children can see their family tree in relation to what else is charted. Draw a parallel line or use a different colored marker for the family history.

Also available for families that have more targeted interests are: TIMETABLES OF™ AMERICAN HISTORY, TIMETABLES OF™ JEWISH HISTORY, TIMETABLES OF™ WOMEN'S HISTORY, TIMETABLES OF™ SCIENCE and TIMETABLES OF™ AFRICAN AMERICAN HISTORY.

I own two encyclopedias — World Book and Britannica. They are both older editions and I refer to them for their history (past, not modern). For quickly changing data, which includes current history, science and technology, a computer with CD Rom encyclopedia, as well as the internet, is the best of all possible worlds.

Why, you might ask, do I prefer older encyclopedias for their history?

All history is slanted based on the facts historians choose to report. They can't report everything — books would be thousands of pages long — so historians must be selective. What they report and what they omit will create the slant. A good explanation of this is found in ARE YOU LIBERAL? CONSERVATIVE? OR CONFUSED?[2] by Richard J. Maybury.

I want to read perspectives that balance those of modern historians. By reading older encyclopedias I am better able to do this. I am currently in the process of acquiring an encyclopedia written circa 1780. It will be interesting to read what historians circa 1780 had to say about the Boston Tea Party, versus today's historians.

A good unabridged dictionary is a necessity. A thesaurus and dictionary are usually built into a good computer word processing program. If you're a history buff, WEBSTER'S 1828 DICTIONARY is a must. This dictionary provides a more accurate definition of words as used at our country's founding. Many words in common use by America's founders cannot be found in modern dictionaries. Many that are found are defined differently now than in 1828. History should be examined in light of the time period as well as in retrospect. Books like WEBSTER'S 1828 DICTIONARY and primary source material help with this.

Remember, any reference book you select must be "user friendly" — it must not overwhelm you to the point that it sits on your shelf collecting dust rather than in your hands.

---

[2] Any resources or books referred to or recommended by the author are listed with publisher's or manufacturer's information in the Directories or the Appendix, of this book.

Academic Resources for Subjects Usually Taught in School

For grammar and writing resources I use Strunk & White's ELEMENTS OF EDITING, ELEMENTS OF STYLE and ELEMENTS OF GRAMMAR.

For math, I recommend BASIC COLLEGE MATHEMATICS by Miller, Salzman and Hestwood, published by Harper. Don't be intimidated by the title. This is a book that was written for college students who didn't understand their math when it was originally taught to them in high school. It begins with whole numbers, works through addition, subtraction, multiplication, division, fractions, decimals, ratio, proportions, percent, measurement, basic algebra, and statistics. It's all the math a noncollege major needs. College prep students would probably want to pursue Introductory and Intermediate Algebra, as well as Geometry, within the same series.

A good science reference is important. One's philosophical foundation, however, would determine which book or books would be placed on your library shelves. Christians usually avoid books with an evolutionary bent, whereas nonChristians tend to avoid the Creationist view. On the other hand, parents from both sides often prefer their children be exposed to both perspectives so opposing viewpoints can be discussed while the student is still in the home. Several catalogs are listed in the appendix that carry resources that support both viewpoints.

Resources for Subjects
Not Commonly Taught in Schools

Models

Children need a model to make sense of the world. The "Uncle Eric" books[3] by Richard J. Maybury provide a model of How the World Works.

What is a model? Mr. Maybury explains:

"One of the most important things you can teach your children is that models are how we think, they are how we understand how the world works. As we go through life we build these very complex pictures in our minds of how the world works, and we're constantly referring back to them—matching incoming data against our models. That's how we make sense of things. One of the most important uses for models is in sorting incoming information to decide if it's important or not.

"In most schools, models are never mentioned because the teachers are unaware of them. One of the most dangerous weaknesses in traditional education is that it contains no model for political history. Teachers teach what they were taught — and no one ever mentioned models to them, so they don't teach them to their students. For the most part, children are just loaded down with collections of facts that they are made to memorize. Without good models, children have no way to know which facts are important and which are not. Students leave school thinking history is a senseless waste of time. Then, deprived of the real lessons of history, the student is vulnerable."

---

[3] For more information on the Uncle Eric books see the listing "Uncle Eric"s Model of How the World Works" on page 90.

The question is, which models to teach. Mr. Maybury says, "the two models that I think are crucially important for everyone to learn are economics and law."

Economics and Law

Most schools don't teach economics or law. Some teach consumer awareness, but little or nothing about business cycles, inflation, recession, etc. Those that do teach economics are most likely to teach Keynesian economics, so if you are free market oriented, as were America's founders, you will need to purchase your own economics books and teach your children yourself. Regarding the subject of justice, America's founders held to an objective standard of truth. Many schools emphasize consensus or decision-making based on the vote of the majority. If you believe in objective truth you will need to provide the instruction yourself.

The best introductory free market economics book available for young people and adults, is WHATEVER HAPPENED TO PENNY CANDY? by Richard Maybury. The best introduction to our country's legal heritage is by the same author, and is titled WHATEVER HAPPENED TO JUSTICE? Together, these books provide the overall model of how human civilization works.

After these books, I recommend ECONOMICS IN ONE LESSON, by Henry Hazlitt published by Crown, NY, and THE LAW by Frederic Bastiat published by the Foundation for Economic Education, Irvington, NY.

Another good book for your family is HOW TO LIE WITH STATISTICS by Darrell Huff, published by W.W. Norton, copyright 1993. One of the best gifts you can give your children is to teach them how to think and how to analyze data.

Additional Subjects

If your religion teaches creationism and your children attend public schools, then the story of creation will need to come from your or your church.

Unless your children attend private school, any religious instruction will need to come from you or through your church, as well.

As school budgets are cut, classes that have been considered elective, will begin to disappear: music, choir, art, drama, and others. You can provide what the school does not. For example, few children will be exposed to classical music. If they hear it and dance to it from the time they are toddlers they have a better chance to develop a love and appreciation for it.

In all of these instances you will need to provide the books, music, etc., to teach what the schools do not.

Primary Source Material

Much emphasis is placed on reading primary source material today. Teach your children that when they read primary source material they are usually reading one person's interpretation of how he or she perceived the world while that person lived. Primary source consists of diaries, journals, letters, first-person accounts,etc. Teach your children that one person's story reflects that person's bias.

To help your children understand this you might explain how difficult it is for you as a parent to discern the truth when your children come to you to help them resolve an argument they are having. You probably begin by having each child tell his or her side of the story, and each child will bias the telling in his or her favor. It doesn't mean they are being dishonest. In the heat of the moment, they are telling you the story the way they see it — each of them.

Primary source material is like this. Authors are reporting their experiences and history as they see it. Ask a Native American and an American cavalryman to each tell his story of what happened at Little Big Horn and you could hardly expect the stories to come out identical. So don't read one diary account about the westward journey overland in 1850. Read several diary accounts. And don't stop at reading a U.S. citizen's account, but also read the Native American's account. This is how you can make primary source material the most useful, and the most representative of an historical event. By presenting different biases your children can learn that truth is somewhere in the midst of all the stories they read.

America's Founders

Read the writings of America's founders. Form your own conclusions based on their actual writings and teach your children to do the same. This is primary source material, and it is biased to their viewpoint — but their philosophy and viewpoint is the philosophy from which America began. By understanding what they said, and not someone's interpretation of what they said, you are better able to determine where and when America has changed course relative to that original philosophy. Whether you agree with the changes that have occurred through the years is a personal determination. But it's essential that you and your children are able to identify the changes. Much is made of what America's founders said, and what they meant, and interpretation has been used by politicians, historians, and religious leaders, to support their own positions today. Someone once said that in a major election, politicians each claim Thomas Jefferson as their own. So, remember, if you don't read for yourself what America's founders said, you subject yourself to someone else's interpretation and bias.

Much of the writings of America's founders have gone out of print. If you find any used books, grab them. Also stock your library from those writings that are available new from publishers before more go out of print.

Guides to Children's Literature

Fifteen years ago, I was familiar with only the most well-known authors of children's literature. When my first child was born I set about to remedy this unfortunate lapse in my education. The Appendix lists many books that can help parents select quality fiction and nonfiction for children. The ISBN that is listed for each book is like a book's social security number. Each edition of a book has it's own ISBN number. This is used for cataloging purposes within the book industry. Any librarian or book store owner is able to locate a book by it's ISBN number.

Visit your public library and browse through as many of these guide books as they have available or can secure through interlibrary loan. You might want to own book guides which are consistent with your philosophical and educational goals. The Appendix lists the philosophical focus of booksellers and authors whenever this information was supplied. For example: Christian, Catholic, secular, home school supplier, etc.

Once you decide which book guide you prefer using, consider buying one or more guides for your home library. Refer to your guides often when making book purchases and your home library should be top quality.

Dewey Decimal System

000-099	General Works (encyclopedias, computer information, journalism)
100-199	Philosophy and Related Disciplines (conduct)
200-299	Religion
300-399	Social Sciences (economics, civics, law, education, vocations)
400-499	Language (language, dictionaries, grammar)
500-599	Pure Sciences (mathematics, physics, chemistry, geology, etc.)
600-699	Technology (medicine, engineering, agriculture, business, etc.)
700-699	The Arts (architecture, sculpture, painting, music, photography)
800-899	Literature (novels, poetry, plays, criticism)
900-999	General Geography and History

4

Organizing Your Home Library

Public libraries use the Dewey Decimal System to catalog their books. You can do the same. The chart on the previous page shows how nonfiction titles are cataloged. In a public library fiction books are organized alphabetically by the author's last name. If the author has more than one title, the books are alphabetized by title. Biographies and autobiographies are usually placed in their own section of the library (nonfiction area). They are alphabetized by the name of the subject. If more than one book on the subject has been written, then they are put in order by the author.

If you want to design your own cataloging system you might want to organize by subject matter, and within a subject heading by age level. For example, one shelf might be devoted to American History, with books arranged by age level. Or you could arrange chronologically by time period. Or you could also arrange by author or title. Organize your home library so that your family will be able to use it. Don't make it too complicated. Look at the ages of your children and decide accordingly.

BOOKS AND LIBRARIES by Jack Knowlton for ages 7-10, explains the evolution of books and the creation of the first libraries — including the Dewey Decimal System.

5

Public and School Libraries

Use of public and school libraries should be reserved for books you don't want or need to own. Borrow books from public or school libraries whose information changes so quickly that it isn't cost effective for you to own the book for the few times you might need to refer to it. Or use these libraries for books that are too expensive to own — many reference books are cost prohibitive for a personal library.

Use of books and use of services are two very different things. You can't replace a helpful librarian. Children's librarians, reference librarians, acquisitions librarians, can be some of your best sources for information. They have the knowledge to help expedite your research. They know what is available in the book and reference world — even though their library might not own it. They know how to help you identify and locate the information you need.

6

Buying Used Inexpensively

Garage Sales,
Moving Sales and Flea Markets

Most of my books have been purchased from private party garage sales. Books are sold very inexpensively from these sources. I normally pay no more than fifty cents for a hardcover book, twenty-five cents for a paperback, and ten cents for a young child's paperback. Once I bought an entire box of children's classics, over twenty-five hardback books, for five dollars.

Generally, if I buy several books from one party I'll make an offer which averages out to less than fifty cents a book. My offer is usually accepted.

The reason for these extraordinary values is that many garage sale shoppers are not interested in buying books, aside from romance novels and the top-ten best sellers. Sellers are not interested in storing books. And if the sale is a moving sale, you might get some real bargains because books are expensive to move.

Once I went to a garage sale that advertised free books. I didn't expect much, but found about twenty volumes of Time-Life books.

Normally I only purchase used books which are in "like new" or "very good" condition. I will buy some children's books in poor condition if I judge they will survive the time my children will use them.

Classified Advertising

Another source for purchasing books is through classified advertising (i.e. newspapers, magazines, newsletter, shopping center classified publications, etc.)

The GREAT BOOKS OF THE WESTERN WORLD by Britannica sell in the neighborhood of $1729.00 (when purchased independently of the BRITANNICA ENCYCLOPEDIA, but at about 50% savings if you have already purchased the BRITANNICA ENCYCLOPEDIA). Since 1990 they added six new volumes. I purchased my set prior to 1990 for $100.00 from a private party, contacting him through a classified ad.

The HARVARD CLASSICS, 51 volumes, are no longer published but are similar to the GREAT BOOKS OF THE WESTERN WORLD. I purchased my set through a classified advertisement for $60.00. I have seen them in a used book store for $70.00.

If you want an encyclopedia that has been recently published, monitor the classified section of the papers. Many times I have seen four to five year-old BRITANNICA ENCYCLOPEDIAS and WORLD BOOK ENCYCLOPEDIAS advertised anywhere from thirty to fifty percent of their original purchase price. In 1985 I purchased a set of the 1977 WORLD BOOK ENCYCLOPEDIA for $60.00 which included all year books through 1984.

Explore your options, especially when looking at large dollar purchases. Compare the number of literature books and other kinds of reference books that can be purchased for the same amount of money needed to buy a new encyclopedia. If you're not certain how frequently your family will use an encyclopedia then you might consider purchasing an older set first. Remember that much of the information in an encyclopedia is historical in content. Purchase a thirty year-old set of BRITANNICA or WORLD BOOK with the intention of using it as a pre-1959 historical reference. People will usu-

ally sell them for five to twenty-five dollars. If you must have a new encyclopedia you can often purchase year-end editions at about 20% discount.

Decide whether your money is better spent on a multi-volume encyclopedia or buying a computer system with CD Rom capabilities (many include an encyclopedia on CD Rom as part of their sales package). You can "surf the internet" and have access to the most immediate data this way.

Newsletters

Subscribe to newsletters which are consistent with your philosophy, special interests, or hobbies. These specialty newsletters often have a classified section where subscribers advertise used books for sale and where you can advertise your willingness to purchase used books.

Thrift Institutions

I purchased an eight year old set of CHILDCRAFT by World Book from a local thrift store for $20.00 plus yearbooks. At that time a new edition of CHILDCRAFT was selling for $199.

Your telephone yellow pages should list consignment stores, second-hand stores, and thrift stores indexed under one of the following headings: Second Hand Dealers, Thrift Shops, or Consignment Services. Telephone or visit these stores and talk with the managers to discover which days the majority of their merchandise arrives at their stores. Ask them the best time to locate books. After Christmas is supposed to be an excellent time for buying used merchandise since many people clean out their wardrobes, toy closets and bookshelves to make room for new items.

Used Book Stores

Another source for purchasing books is a used book store. Books may be discounted up to 50% of the book's retail price. You must visit used book stores regularly in order to improve your chances of finding good books. For a small fee some store owners will maintain a list of books their customers want. They will purchase these books when given the opportunity and hold them in your name.

Retiring Teachers

I knew a teacher who had helped develop the curriculum for a small private school which had disbanded. I was able to find many books and instructional aids in her garage which she sold at a fraction of their original cost.

Call the schools in your area and find out if the school has any teachers who are retiring. If so, ask those teachers if they have any materials or books for sale.

Home School Curriculum Fairs

Many home school organizations (state, regional, and local) sponsor conferences and curriculum fairs. Depending on the organization, a used book section can be part of the exhibit hall. Query to find out if your home school organization has this option available. Also ask if "an exhibit hall only" pass is available, which lets you into the exhibit hall for a substantially lower fee than it would cost if you were to sign up for the entire conference (including workshops, keynote speakers, etc.). Some vendors will sell at discount in these exhibit halls. Query exhibit hall coordinators to determine if they are allowing discount sellers to exhibit in their exhibit hall. Some permit this and others exclude discount vendors. Some organizations sponsor a used curriculum fair separate from the main conference to prevent conflicts in the exhibit hall.

To find out more about home school organizations in your area, contact one of the national home school organizations listed on page 86.

Book Sales

Private schools conduct book sales to generate revenues for the school. Books purchased at these sales may be up to twice the price of books purchased at garage and moving sales, but oftentimes you can find a better quality of books from which to choose than from garage sales. In addition, there are so many books from which to select that there is the advantage of not having to drive to a number of different places to locate moderately priced books.

Book sales are also conducted by Friends of the Library organizations. These books are sold at garage sale prices or even less. In my town these sales are conducted monthly. Telephone your librarian to determine the frequency of your library's used book sales.

Note also that some libraries have shelves of discarded books which are sold for twenty-five cents to a dollar.

Public school book depositories also conduct public book sales. You are apt to find many used and worn textbooks which the district has replaced with new books. Sometimes books that have never been used are sold. Prices are cheap.

Auctions and Estate Sales

Monitor the classified section of the newspaper, under the Auction subheading, to learn when estate sales and auctions will be held. Sometimes estate sales are advertised under the Garage Sale subheading.

Of the three types of estate sales, the first is run like a garage sale, and items are usually priced accordingly. The second might be handled by an auctioneer or appraiser, but is a tagged sale, in which all prices are predetermined by the owner, auctioneer, and/or executor. The third is an auction at which items put up for sale are sold to the highest bidder. Sometimes a minimum bid will be posted, and items will only be sold if someone bids above the minimum.

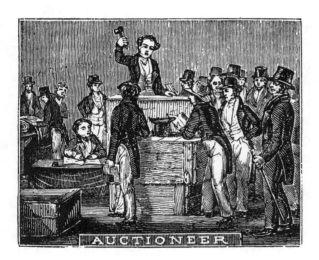

Telephone the owner/auctioneer and inquire if books are part of the estate, and if so, what types of books are being sold. With luck, you can do some valuable previewing over the telephone. Then decide if a follow-up visit to the auction site is in order. If books you want to add to your library are part of the sale, inquire if absentee bid forms are available. Fill out a form indicating your bid price and the auctioneer will enter your bid at the appropriate time. If yours is the highest bid, you get the books. The absentee form eliminates the need for your sitting through a long auction when you are only interested in one item. Note that books are usually sold in lots, and you can bid on one or more lots. Determine which books in the lot are those you want for your home library, figure what price you are willing to pay for just those books, and submit that price. If yours is the highest bid you can dispose of the unwanted books at a resale store, used book store, charity, or your own garage sale.

Networking

If you are looking for particular books, let anyone who's willing to help you know your needs. This includes friends, family, and colleagues. Contact your librarians, church members, club or association members, etc. I told my reference librarian I was looking for a set of THE ANNALS OF AMERICA published by Britannica. This multi-volume series is an anthology of primary source material. Volume One begins in 1493 and my set goes through 1968. Since my research usually encompasses the years 1450 to 1950, this met my needs perfectly. My cost was $20 for the set. A current edition runs $499.

Volunteer at Your Library

Some libraries allow their volunteers to have the first option of buying any books that are donated to the library for fund raising before they are made available to the public. Ask about this anytime you volunteer to work at a used book sale or book fundraiser.

7

Buying New Inexpensively

Book Stores

One of the most expensive sources of new books is the retail book store that sells at full retail price. Many retail book stores, however, do carry some discounted or remaindered books. Many of the chains have bargain sections or are known as a discount chain. Check your telephone yellow pages. Also check the "Directory of Resources for Stocking a Home Library Inexpensively" in this book for listings of stores that sell at discount.

Discount Catalogs

Over 80 catalogs that always sell at discount, or offer volume discounts, or bundle certain products for special price savings are listed in the "Directory of Resources for Stocking a Home Library Inexpensively" located in this book. A description of their products, discount policy and guarantee is included whenever this information was provided.

Remainders, Close-outs, and Publisher's Overstocks

Some people are under the mistaken notion that books sold as remainders are of inferior quality (content speaking) which accounts for the reason they were unsuccessfully sold at full retail price. Perhaps this is the case once in a while. But many remainders are acquired because the publisher misjudged the quantity he could sell (even if this is the publisher's twentieth printing of a best-selling title). One might think of the remainder dealer as equivalent to "a sale" — it's the publisher's effort to move his inventory.

Why would a remainder dealer want to purchase a book that isn't selling? Book buying consumers make up three different groups: hardcover buyers, paperback buyers and bargain buyers. Booksellers specializing in remainders and overstocks are in business to sell to that third group — bargain buyers.

Book Clubs

A book offered through a book club is usually less expensive than its original retail price. Some book club programs require members to purchase a certain number of books within a specified period of time. Other clubs offer a program in which you are under no obligation to purchase any books. An editor's choice is made monthly. You must notify the book club if you do not want the selected book. Otherwise you will receive both the book and a bill in the mail.

Those book clubs that responded to my query are listed in the directory section called "Directory of Resources for Stocking a Home Library Inexpensively."

THE ENCYCLOPEDIA OF ASSOCIATIONS published by Gale Research and R.R. Bowkers's LITERARY MARKET PLACE each list a far more comprehensive list of book clubs. Just a few of the categories listed include: art, health, literature, science, science fiction, children's books, real estate, photography, history, music, educators, how-to, romance, cooking, nature, Catholic, Christian, among others. See if your library carries these reference books.

Work for a Library or Bookstore

If you work for a library or bookstore you may be permitted to purchase books, cassettes, CD's and videos at the library or store's cost. Ask.

Promotions

Companies will sometimes offer promotions whereby you receive a free book by sending in "proofs of purchase" from a product. Watch for these offers.

Warehouse Stores

Books sold at warehouse stores are often sold at wholesale price. These stores buy in huge quantities and get deep discounts. If you can purchase a book at 40% off its cover price, you are usually buying at a wholesale level. Keep the 40% off rule in mind as a guideline whenever you are pricing books.

Educational Discounts

If your home is registered or incorporated as a private school you may be eligible for a school or educator's discount. Several companies offer educational discounts. Whenever you purchase a new book, instructional aide, art supplies, or computer equipment or software, be sure to inquire if an educator's discount is available.

As the home school market continues to grow, more companies are developing special programs to meet the needs of this market. For example, Scholastic Book Clubs, which used to service schools, now includes home school buyers in their clubs. You'll notice some other companies listed in the Appendix that have also made special provisions to service home school families.

Book Parties

Educators Publishing Corporation (also known as Usborne Books) has a book party plan. You host the party and receive books as your compensation. Check the "Directory of Resources for Stocking a Home Library Inexpensively" for their listing to write for more information.

8

Buying New at Full Retail Price

The idea behind this book has been to provide you with as many ideas and sources for purchasing books inexpensively as I could discover. Hopefully, if books are more affordable, people will have more incentive for developing a home library — especially parents.

You won't always be able to find every book you want or need for your home library at discount. Occasionally you will have to buy new.

Beginning on page 61 is a "Directory of Resources for Stocking a Home Library Conveniently." Always remember that time is money. The catalogs listed in this section are listed for your convenience — for your armchair shopping — to save you time, gas, and wear and tear on your automobile.

They will also save you from making purchasing errors, since many of these catalogs provide extensive product reviews.

Whenever possible, I have listed the catalog's philosophical orientiation, catalog focus, speciality area when appropriate, and age levels targeted.

Several of these catalog companies were established to service the rapidly expanding home school market. Consequently, they have gone way beyond the focus of most book catalogs which have traditionally sold literature. These home school catalogs provide products for every academic subject.

A section in the appendix called "Home School Favorites" lists learning resource guides and literature guides that have stood the test of time with home school parents.

Gifts

Some books might seem like luxury items. They might be too expensive for an everyday purchase. So, reserve birthdays and all other gift-giving occasions for books you wouldn't usually buy.

9

Making Money or Breaking Even When It's Time to Sell Your Books

When I'm ready to dispose of books, often because my children have outgrown them, I do so in one of four ways.

1. I sell them myself at a garage sale, in which case I might break even on my investment.

2. I sell or trade them to a used book store.

3. I put them on consignment at a children's resale shop, in which case I usually make money.

4. I sell them through a home school network, in which case I make money. Home school curriculum fairs, mentioned earlier, are also places to sell used books.

The last two options are ones to keep in mind when you are buying books for your home library. If you find books at garage sale prices which you already have, don't think of them as duplicates. Think of them as a way to subsidize your home library. Put them on consignment at children's resale stores or try finding a special interest group, like home school families, that would jump at the chance to own these books. Usually you can make a profit and the buyers are also happy because they have purchased books for substantially lower prices than retail.

10

Subsidizing the Cost of Your Home Library

If you are combing through classified ads looking for used books (usually the miscellaneous column), as well as garage sale advertisements, keep your eyes open for other bargains.

Used clothing for young children can be found very inexpensively at garage sales and, if purchased, will generate huge savings in the family clothing budget. Name brand cord slacks can be purchased for one dollar, shirts for fifty cents, socks for one nickel. Only buy clothing which is in very good condition. Be willing to buy ahead for clothes that your children will grow into.

Toys are another savings area. I purchased $30 worth of plastic building blocks for fifty cents at a garage sale. A name-brand hobby vise, worth about $22, was purchased for twenty-five cents. I found a trolley cable ride that had never been used which sells new for about $32 — I paid three dollars. Wood puzzles can be purchased for seventy-five cents. Action figures can be found for twenty-five cents to one dollar. And the list goes on. Add it up, the savings are tremendous!

Consider buying your furniture used. I have purchased used furniture that is in like new condition. We have a burgundy leather chair in our bedroom that sells new for about $1000. We paid $300.

Purchase office equipment used. My first computer was purchased used, but was so new it was still within the manufacturer's warranty period, so the gamble was almost nonexistent and the savings — substantial.

How about tools? I purchased a name-brand tool chest in excellent condition for my husband for $50 that would have cost $300 new. A shredder/chipper was purchased for $75 that would have cost $500 new. And the list goes on.

Small items: A sprinkler can for ten cents rather than two dollars. Children's garden tools (a real rake and hoe) for three dollars rather than $20.

Don't be afraid to ask for merchandise you are looking for if it isn't displayed at a garage sale. It's amazing what people will bring from their houses and barns if they have what you want.

Money you save by shopping for used furniture, tools, clothing, toys, etc., can be used to purchase books for your home library.

Some people use their "coupon money" for buying books. Whatever money they save by using coupons, they put towards their book budget.

What about selling materials that are no longer useful to you? The WHERE TO SELL IT DIRECTORY published by Pilot Book, lists sources that might be interested in buying what you have to sell, including: art, Americana, autographs, letters, automobile parts, badges, aviation items, Christmas items, games, lunch boxes, pottery, railroad items and much more. The listings are mostly comprised of collectors.

"Books that List Cost-Saving Ideas, Where to Buy Free or at Discount" begins on page 87 of the Appendix. Money saved by following these suggestions can be put toward subsidizing the home library.

11

Three Rules for Shopping Used

Three rules to remember when shopping used are:

1. Plan ahead.
2. Have patience to wait for items that are either in like new condition or in very good condition.
3. Pay what the item is worth to you.

By planning ahead you determine what the needs of your family will be. One child may be wearing size four pants next Winter, but size three shorts in the Spring. It might be two years before your child will be old enough to play with a particular board game, but at fifty cents it's worth storing on a shelf. Although your child might be looking at picture books now, a set of children's classics will be a cherished possession in a few short years.

Buy ahead and store bargains. By doing this you can be much more selective about what you will buy now and what you will pass over, knowing you have plenty of time to find the best used merchandise before the need for it materializes.

A rule of thumb I use when shopping used is to pay no more than 25% of an item's retail value new. If I pay less, I figure I have captured a bargain. The rule of thumb for "a real bargain" is to pay no more than what the sales tax would be if I purchased the item new. For example, if a toy sells new for $4.50, the sales tax on this would be twenty-eight cents. Twenty-five cents would be a real bargain.

Remember, bargaining is part of the fun and usually expected. Without the willingness of yourself and others like you to buy used merchandise, the garage sale entrepreneurs would make no sales.

12

Happy Hunting!

You should now know:

1. Why a home library is important.

2. How to decide which books you want to purchase.

3. Where to purchase them — inexpensively!

You may even be able to make money at this activity if you plan, have patience and pay the right price. **Happy Hunting!**

Afterword

If you know of other ways to reduce the cost of book purchases please write Jane Williams in care of Bluestocking Press, P.O. Box 1014, Dept. 3H, Placerville, California, 95667-1014. New ideas will be added to future revisions of HOW TO STOCK A HOME LIBRARY INEXPENSIVELY. If your idea is used in a subsequent issue, and you are the first to submit the idea, you will receive one complimentary copy of the revised edition.

Directory of
Resources
for
Stocking a Home Library
Inexpensively

Alliance for Parental Involvement in Education, Inc. (ALLPIE)
established 1989
95% home schoolers
Katharine Houk
P.O. Box 59
East Chatham, NY 12060
Phone: 518-392-6900
E-mail: America Online: ALLPIE SR.
Internet: allpiesr@aol.com. From
Compuserve: >INTERNET
allpiesr@aol.com
All-inclusive adult catalog

> Allpie Book & Resources Catalog targets parents. Catalog focus: resources to help parents know their educational options and become involved—public, private and home schooling.
> **Discount:** ALLPIE offers a 10% discount to members at the Associate and Sustaining levels ($40 and up). ALLPIE offers a 15% discount for books which will be used in a lending library of partner groups.
> **Guarantee:** Money-back or credit guarantee for items returned in salable condition.

Alpha Omega Publications
established 1977
Bob J. Campbell, President
404 W. 21st
P.O. Box 3153
Tempe, AZ 85282
Phone: 602-438-2717; 800-821-4443
Fax: 602-438-2702
Christian catalog

> Annual direct mail catalog of PreK-12: Catalog of Home Learning. Christian curriculum and ancillary educational products for the home and school. Contains products from over 70 Christian and secular manufacturers. Also has the

Bridgestone Multimedia Catalog.
Discount: Offers a Spring Sale: 25% off every order over $150; 15% off every order from $50-$150 (before shipping/ handling and applicable sales tax).

Anthroposophic Press
established 1928
5% home schoolers
Greg Richey, Marketing Manager
RR 4 Box 94A-1
Hudson, NY 12534
Phone: 518-851-2054
Fax: 518-851-2047
Waldorf catalog

> Publisher of books on education, Waldorf education, family life, children's activities and crafts, children's books; wholistic approach to child development.
> **Discount:** 15% Christmas discount: October 15-December 31, every year.
> **Guarantee:** Full money back guarantee.

Apologetics Press
Dr. Bert Thompson
Marketing Director — Retail Sales
230 Landmark Drive
Montgomery, AL 36117
Phone: 800-234-8558
Fax: 334-270-2002
Christian.

> DISCOVERY, a monthly paper of Bible and science for grade school children.
> **Discount:** Home school discounts: 1-2 subscriptions: $9.00 each; 3 or more to same address: $6.50 each; 10 or more to different addresses paid together: $7.50 each; $11.00 per year for 12 monthly issues.
> **Guarantee:** Satisfaction guaranteed.

Applegate's Little Red Schoolhouse
40% home schoolers
Paulette or Jim Applegate
4100 Cameron Park Drive, #111
Cameron Park, CA 95682
Phone: 916-672-2227
Fax: 916-672-1805
School and home school educational supply
store (1000 sq. ft. of retail space)
> Targeting preschool through high school.
> Serves public and private classroom
> educators, home schools/alternative
> educators and families. 40% home
> schoolers; 10% private educators. Cata-
> log projected 1995. Expanded inventory
> of used curriculum. Carries Christian and
> secular material.
> **Discount:** $10.00 store credit for every
> $100.00 in-store purchases (some exclu-
> sions apply). Various volume discounts
> will be offered in catalog.

Barb's People Builders
established 1992
97% home schoolers
Barbara Radisavjevic
3420 Hwy 46W
Templeton, CA 93465
Phone: 805-237-9639
Fax: 805-237-9639
Christian, all-inclusive specialty catalog
> PreK-high school. Catalog focus: his-
> tory, foreign language, language arts,
> hands-on science, classic literature.
> Specialist in history and children's
> literature, and foreign languages.
> **Discount:** Volume discount. $100 cash
> or check qualifies for 10% discount.
> **Guarantee:** Products guaranteed.

Barbour & Co. Inc.
established 1981
Hugh R. Barbour, President
1810 Barbour Drive
Uhrichsville, OH 44683
Phone: 614-922-6045
Fax: 614-922-5948
Christian
> Publisher of bargain books: Christian
> literature.

Barnes & Noble
Fred Eisenhart, Sales Director
One Pond Road
Rockleigh, NJ 07647
Phone: 201-767-6660   800-242-6657
Fax: 201-784-4213
Catalog
> Sells publishers' remainders & hardcover
> reprints to trade, institutional & foreign
> markets. Specialize in art, biography,
> history, literature & quality fiction.
> Warehouse: Thousands of titles. Also
> trade HC and PB and imports. Catalog
> sales only.
> **Discount:** Some savings up to 80%.
> **Guarantee:** Satisfaction is guaranteed.

Beginning of Wisdom
established 1992
25% home schoolers
Craig McAllister
54 Plumb Hill Road, Dept. BHL 9503
Washington, CT 06793
Phone: 203-868-9557
Christian catalog and store
> General education. Discounts on family
> videos, books, music (cassettes and CD's
> for families and children), science and
> carpentry kits, home decorations, how-to
> booklets, ideas for saving money, and
> much more. Age group: 1-100. "The
> fear of the Lord is the beginning of
> wisdom." (Psalm 111.10)

Beginning of Wisdom—continued
Discount: Many of our items are discounted, and we also have sales. Please reference this listing to receive a free catalog.
Guarantee: Satisfaction guaranteed.

Berkshire Record Outlet, Inc.
Joe Ekstein
Rural Route 1
Lee, MA   01238
Phone: 800-992-1200; 413-243-4080
Fax: 413-243-4340
Catalog and store
Remaindered and overstocks: LP's, cassettes, classical music and musicians' works. Store open Saturdays only, 11:30 am - 5:30 pm. Catalog is 188 pages. Cost: $2.00. For steady customers it is sent free of charge.
Guarantee: Defective items may be exchanged for identical items with copy of the receipt within one year.

Bird Book Source
established 1990
Arnold K. Brown, President
Box 1088
Vineyard Haven, MA 02568
Phone: 508-693-4811 800-443-4811
Fax: 508-693-6311
E-mail: OSPREY@TIAC.NET
Adult book club
Books about birds and birding. No charge to join, but we stop mailing if you do not buy in a reasonable time.
Discount: 12% on all orders once you purchase $100 in each calendar year.

Bks.
Marketing Director — Retail Sales
Paperback Avenue
Charlotteville, NY 12036
Phone: 800-854-8508   607-397-8389
Catalog
Sells paperbacks to schools and individuals outside New York State.
Discount: 0-24 books = No discount; 25-250 books = 20% discount; 251-999 books = 25% discount; 1000-2999 books = 30% discount; 3000+ books = 33% discount; 5000+ books = Call for Quote. Individuals must prepay.

Bluestocking Press
established 1987
80% home schoolers
Jane Williams
P.O. Box 1014 - Dept. hl3
Placerville, CA 95667-1014
Phone: 800-959-8586; 916-622-8586
Fax: 916-642-9222
All-inclusive PreK through adult specialty catalog
Major emphasis: American history, free market economics and higher law, with sections on performing arts, writing, critical thinking, and mathematics. History is arranged chronologically by time period and within that time period by age or grade level. Includes: fiction, nonfiction, primary source material, historical music, historical documents, historical toys and more. First class shipping of the resource guide and catalog is available for $3.00. Bulk mail shipping is available at no charge, but occurs once a year in the Spring, when resource guide and catalog is reprinted.
Discount: Items they publish are eligible for a discount when purchased in bulk or purchased at a bundled price. Certain catalog items are bundled for savings.

Guarantee: If for any reason an item does not meet with customer's satisfaction it can be returned within 30 days for a full refund. Exceptions: No refunds on audio, video products or games if packaging has been removed unless the item is defective. Shipping charges are not refunded unless the item is defective. Special order items are not returnable.

Book Beat Ltd.

Cary Loren, Owner
26010 Greenfield Road
Oak Park, MI 48237
Phone: 810-968-1190
Fax: 810-968-3102
E-mail: Bookbeat@aol.com or caryloren@delphi.com
Catalog, store and book club
Primarily adult catalog. Books, specializing in art, photography, & some children's. Also original vintage photographs.
Discount: 10%-20% on most hardcovers.

Book Cellar

established 1991
David Graceffa, General Manager
87 Union Square
Milford, NH 03055
Phone: 603-672-4333
E-mail: NEE Books @ aol, com
Christian store, remainder
Used home school curriculum. K-12. Some titles for adults. College textbooks used. Technical Books. Used and New (advanced professions). Visa, MC, Discover cards accepted.
Discount: 25-75% off list.

Book Explosion

established 1979
Trish Weyd, Marketing Director — Retail Sales
2039 Wilton Drive
Ft. Lauderdale, FL 33305
Phone: 305-564-2499; 800-443-2559
Fax: 305-565-4786
Christian store
Books and Bibles at discount. Call for bid on quantity purchases of pew Bibles, hymnals, books & church supplies.
Discount: New materials at discount. Minimum discounts start at 20%. Phone for quotes beyond that.

Booksmith Promotional Co.

established 1973
Phil Hochberg, President
100 Paterson Blank Road
Jersey City, NJ 07307
Phone: 718-782-0405; 201-659-2768, 2317
Fax: 201-659-3631
Remainders
Promotional assortments to trade & institutional markets. Specialize in art, juveniles, quality paperbacks, textbooks, psychology & general nonfiction titles. Warehouse: 5000 titles.
Discount: 50% discount.

Builder Books

established 1984
95% home schoolers
Patty Alberg, Buyer
HC 65 Box 104N
PO Box 99
Riverside, WA 98849
Phone: 509-826-6021
Christian all-inclusive catalog
Preschool through high school, emphasis on elementary.
Discount: Asterisk next to catalog item denotes discounted price. Volume

Builder Books — continued

discount is now applied directly to each item. No more volume required. Free shipping on some items not discounted.
Guarantee: Money back guarantee/30 days.

C. J. Huff Books
established 1989
95% home schoolers
Cindy Huff, Owner
371 Beach St.
Aurora, IL 60505
Phone: 708-851-8206
Catalog
Discount prices, including: Unit study, Christian biographies, math, grammar, writing, Saxon math, Easy Grammar, fiction, art, history, Moody science videos, Christian Liberty Books, Ruth Beechick, Light & Glory series, Unit Study Material, and more.
Discount: Discount catalog. Secure a copy of the catalog.

Cahill & Co.
Director of Marketing
PO Box 64554
St. Paul, MN 55114-0554
Phone: 800-755-8531; 612-659-3700
Catalog
Sells at discount.

Children's Books
established 1985
95% home schoolers
Barbara Lopez, Director of Marketing
P.O. Box 19069
Denver, CO 80219
Phone: 303-237-4989
All-inclusive catalog
Preschool through high school. All subject matter.

Discount: 20-30% off on all books sold depending on quantity.
Guarantee: Full refund if not satisfied.

Children's Bookshop
established 1988
30% home schoolers
Bob or Sara Carter Beavers, Marketing Director
225 W. Meeker St.
Kent, WA 98032
Phone: 206-852-0383
All-inclusive store
General education. K-8, all educational subject areas.
Discount: 20% discount on children's books.
Guarantee: Exchanges with a receipt within 30 days.

Children's Corner Bookshop
5-8% home schoolers
Judy Hamel
Susan Durrie
814 West Maine
Spokane, WA 99201
Phone: 509-624-4820
Store
Over 15,000 titles. Literature and educational books birth through grade 12.
Discount: Home schoolers receive 10% discount on full-priced purchases.

Christian Book Bargains
Mary Burns, Marketing Director — Retail Sales
PO Box 1009
Dover, OH 44622
Phone: 800-221-2648
Fax: 800-220-5948
Christian catalog
Christian Book Bargains' mail order catalog includes: Bibles; fiction; greeting cards; videos and music; children's

books, tapes, videos and activity books; Christian comics (all are Christian books).

Discount: Christian Book Bargains advertise savings of up to 90%. Shipping and handling is a flat $2.00. Pay in U.S. Dollars. Foreign orders add $5.00 to cover increased cost of postage and documents.

Guarantee: "All books in this catalog are guaranteed to please, whether purchased for your own enjoyment or given as gifts to friends. Because we care about our customers and want to insure your satisfaction, you may return any purchase within 30 days for a full refund."

Christian Book Distributors

established 1978
Marketing Director — Retail Sales
Box 7000
Peabody, MA 01961-7000
Phone: 508-977-5000
Fax: 508-977-5010
Christian / Catholic catalog

Christian Book Distributors carries more than 10,000 titles (and growing) from over 200 top publishers like Word, Zondervan, Baker, Nelson, and more. Sells: Bibles, commentaries, Greek and Hebrew reference works, preaching and pastoral resources, youth ministry resources, church and Bible history references, marriage and parenting, personal development, Bible study tools, fiction, bestsellers, children's books, videos, games, music, computer software, CD-ROM, classics and biographies, devotionals, and more. Phone weekdays 7 a.m. to midnight (EST) and Saturdays 9 a.m. to 5 p.m. (EST).

Discount: Save up to 60% off retail on almost every title; save up to 90% on close-out items. CBD Membership is optional; however, members are guaranteed lowest prices available: USA $5.00/year; Canada $5.00/year; International $8.00/year. Members receive all catalogs, including membership newsletters and special sales notices. Payment must accompany order. MC/Visa/Discover Card accepted.

Guarantee: No returns permitted unless books received are damaged, defective or shipped in error.

Christian Curriculum Cellar

established 1992
90% home schoolers
Georgene & Kevin Girouard
4460 S. Carpenter Rd.
Modesto, CA 95358
Phone: 209-538-3632
Christian catalog

New and used books, K-12. All major publishers. Phone 1:00-4:00 p.m. M-F.
Discount: 25%-75% off retail.
Trade-ins accepted towards curriculum.

Christian Discount Book Center

Marketing Director — Retail Sales
8401 S. Pioneer Blvd.
Whittier, CA 90606
Phone: 310-692-1296
Fax: 310-695-6991
Christian bookstore

4 store locations: 1010 E. Arrow Hwy. at Grand Ave., Covina, CA 91724, 818-967-2893; 714 S. Rancho Santa Fe Rd. at San Marcos Blvd., San Marcos, CA 619-727-5860; 16595 Magnolia St. off the 405 Fwy., Westminster, CA, 714-847-0396.
Discount: Regularly 5-20% off retail. Westminster store is an outlet store with savings up to 90%.

Christian Liberty Press
established 1968
Michael McHugh
502 West Euclid Avenue
Arlington Heights, IL 60004
Phone: 708-259-8736; 800-832-2741
Christian catalog
   A full line of general education subjects:
   phonics, reading, handwriting, spelling,
   grammar, mathematics, Bible, Christian
   biographies, history, science, govern-
   ment, economics at discount prices.
   Discount: Discounts on Christian Liberty Press products only. Quantity orders
   in the 11-30 book range have a 30%
   discount. Orders that contain 31 or more
   Christian Liberty Press products get a
   40% discount.
   Guarantee: All items ordered from our
   catalog can be returned for a refund or
   credit within thirty days. A ten percent
   restocking fee is applied to all returns.

Christian Teaching Materials Company
established 1987
98% home schoolers
Kathy Motto
P.O. Box 639
14275 Elm Ave.
Glenpool, OK 74033
Phone: 918-322-3420
Christian catalog and store
   100 page catalog, $1.00. Thousands of
   products with detailed product descriptions. New educational materials, some at
   discount prices. Targeted age group: K-
   12.
   Discount: Discounts on close-outs, out
   of print books and special buys.
   Guarantee: If you are not satisfied with
   a product you may return it within 14
   days of receipt for a refund or exchange.
   It must be in brand new, resalable condi-

tion. It must be returned either by UPS,
RPS, or post office insured. Enclose your
packing slip highlighting any items
returned. Shipping and handling charges
are not refundable or credited. This
guarantee does not apply to discontinued,
on sale, or out of print products.

Chula Vista Books
established 1993
60% home schoolers
Teah McWhorter
420 Chula Vista Mountain Rd.
Pell City, AL 35125
Phone: 205-338-1843
Christian catalog and store
   Sells new products at discount. Chula
   Vista Books' purpose is to provide as
   many of the good resources and curricu-
   lums as they can at a discount price.
   Also carry large supply of Bible study
   materials and helps. Pre-K through adult
   level catalog, biannual. Catalog focus:
   educational materials and supplies,
   religious materials.
   Discount: Approximately 10% discount
   on most products, no minimum.
   Guarantee: Query for return policy.

Classics Club
established 1989
Herbert J. Kohen, Director
311 Crossways Park Drive
Woodbury, NY 11797
Phone: 516-364-1800
Adult book club
   Hardcover classics.

Conservative Book Club
established 1964
Maureen McCaffrey
33 Oakland Ave.
Harrison, NY 10528

Book club

Every 4 weeks (13 times a year) you get a free copy of the Club Bulletin which offers you the Featured Selection plus a good choice of Alternates—all of interest to conservatives and parents. If you want the Featured Selection, do nothing, it will come automatically. If you don't want the Featured Selection, or you do want an Alternate, indicate your wishes on the card which comes with your Bulletin and return it by the deadline dates.

Discount: The majority of Club books will be offered at 20-50% discounts, plus a charge for shipping and handling. The Club will offer regular Super bargains, mostly at 70-90% discounts plus shipping and handling. Super bargains do NOT count toward fulfilling your Club obligation, but do enable you to buy fine books at giveaway prices.Only one membership per household.

Guarantee: If you ever receive a Featured Selection without having had 10 days to decide if you want it, you may return it at Club expense for full credit.

Cornerstone Books
established 1991
80-85% home schoolers
Jim or Deb McBride
10819 NE 179th St.
Battle Ground, WA 98604-9456
Phone: 800-487-5952
Fax: 360-687-6920
E-mail: Prodigy
GSSD22A@PRODIGY.COM
Christian catalog and store

K-12, all subjects, Christian books and home school supplies, music and video tapes. Christian bookstore gearing toward home school customer. Annual catalog published in March.

Discount: 0-$100 = Free shipping; $100-$200 = Free shipping plus 10% discount; $200+ = Free shipping plus 15% discount

Guarantee: Money back if not satisfied within 30 days, if merchandise is undamaged.

Creative Kids Learning Company
established 1983
99% home schoolers
Naomi Strunk, Owner
964 Holland Road
Holland, PA 18966
Phone: 215-355-5834
All-inclusive catalog and store

Sells home school curriculum and materials by mail. Targets ages K-12; focus on curriculum and supplementary educational materials. Send for FREE current sale listing. Free shipping on Saxon and Sing, Spell, Read & Write with mention of this ad. In-home display room open Saturday 1:00-5:00 PM. Call Saturday 1:00-5:00 PM for curriculum consultation.

Discount: Certain items always discounted. Sales on other products vary.
Guarantee: If you are not completely satisfied, return item in NEW condition, in original wrapping within 15 days, and we will return your money.

Curriculum Cottage
established 1992
99% home schoolers
Cynthia Sciscoe
2210 N. Meridian Rd.
Meridian, ID 83642
Phone: 208-887-9292
Christian nonsectarian catalog and store

Targets adults with children. Focus: Complete curriculum for home education.

Curriculum Cottage—continued

Distributes to home school & parents wishing to supplement current form of education. Distributes in all required subject areas.

Discount: Many products priced below retail. All Bible curriculum 10% off.

D.P. & K. Productions

established 1993
Pat Wesolowski
2201 High Rd.
Tallahassee, FL 32303
Phone: 904-385-1958
Christian specialty catalog

Big Ideas Small Budget newsletter full of money-making and money-saving ideas. $12 for 11 issues per year. Free subscription with ideas published. Sample issue: $1.00 + SASE. Book of same title: $10.00 - compilation of back issues. INFORMATION, PLEASE! - Research curriculum supplement, 4 levels - $15.00 + 1.50 S&H. Catalog will be forthcoming. $2.00 off with mention of HOW TO STOCK A HOME LIBRARY INEXPENSIVELY.

Daedalus Books

established 1980
Helaine Harris, Vice-President
PO Box 9132
Hyattsville, MD 20781-0932
Phone: 800-395-2665; Customer service # 800-944-8879 (9AM-6PM EST).
Fax: 800-866-5578
Catalog

Books include: Literature & general interest; gardening; publishing; audio books; travel books; children's books; visual & performing arts; Italian sculp-

ture; philosophy; history; social & political sciences; physical & natural sciences; remainders. All orders must be prepaid. Ten dollars minimum for charge card orders.

Discount: Daedalus' mail-order catalog advertises "fine sale books from trade publishers and university presses at 50-90% off."

Guarantee: "If you are in any way dissatisfied with your purchase, you may return the book(s) for a full refund or exchange. We welcome returns within a 30 day period."

Detective Book Club

established 1942
Herbert J. Kohen, President
311 Crossways Park Drive
Woodbury, NY 11797
Phone: 516-364-1800
Adult book club

Hardcover mysteries, 3 novels in one binding.

Devin-Adair Publishers Inc.

established 1911
Chris Dowdell, Customer Service Manager
6 N. Water Street
Greenwich, CT 06830
Phone: 203-531-7755
Adult Christian

Books relating to health, gardening, foods, politics, Irish literature and American history. Hardcover and paperbacks.

Discount: 20% store or library discount.

Guarantee: If book is paid for and buyer is dissatisfied, full refund of price of book is given.

Dover Publications
Paul Negri
31 East 2nd St.
Mineola, NY 11501
Phone: 516-294-7000
Catalog

Dover specializes in copyright-free art, but publishes in many fields with over 6,000 books in print. They sell books on art instruction, crafts, fine art, posters, postcards, books for children (stencils, activity books, models, mazes, dot-to-dot, coloring books, paper dolls, dioramas, masks), postcards, music, mathematics, physics, engineering, stickers, seals, language, learning and linguistics, and photographs. They offer hundreds of books for just $1.00 each — from literary classics (Dover Thrift Editions) to iron-on transfers. Although they are not a discount book seller or remainder dealer, their books are very reasonably priced and their catalog worth browsing.
Guarantee: "All Dover books are unconditionally guaranteed and may be returned (with the original order if possible) within 10 days of receipt for full cash refund. No questions asked."

Drinking Gourd, The
established 1992
95% home schoolers
Donna Nichols-White, Editor
P.O. Box 2557
Redmond, WA 98073
Phone: 206-836-0330
Fax: 206-868-1371
All-inclusive children and adult catalog

Catalog: THE DRINKING GOURD BOOK CO.; age group: K-college. Focus: educational-independent learning.
Discount: Some products sold at discount.

Education Connection
established 1993
98% home schoolers
Lori Schall
P.O. Box 1417
Tehachapi, CA 93581
Phone: 805-823-8022
All-inclusive children's catalog

New at discount. Early learning through grade eight, all subject areas. Nearly every item is priced below suggested retail prices.
Guarantee: Unconditional money back guarantee - customer may inspect materials for 10 days. Refunded or credited for item, but not shipping and handling.

Education Station
David and Julene Humes
1395 North 400 East
Pleasant Grove, UT 84062
Phone: 801-785-1466
Catalog

Discount materials for the educating home.

Educational Preferred Services
established 1975
30-40% home schoolers
Betty Brewer
Cheylnn Sadler
1129 Garden Gate Circle
Garland, TX 75043
Phone: 214-278-9961
All-inclusive catalog

Assist with curriculum planning. K-12, all subject areas, strongest in language arts. Mainstream classroom. Open to all subject areas, no Biblically based materials.

Edward R. Hamilton, Bookseller
Marketing Director — Retail Sales
Falls Village, CT 06031-5000
Catalog
>   Over 40 subject areas.
>   **Discount:** Save 50%-80%.

Emeth Educational Supplies
established 1994
95% home schoolers
Carol Saia, Owner
20618 Cypress Way
Lynnwood, WA 98036
Phone: 206-672-8708
Christian catalog and store
>   All subjects. Specializes in home school-
>   ing materials, but also includes many
>   books and educational games of interest
>   to students in traditional schools.
>   **Discount:** Many items discounted 10%
>   below retail price. Volume discount of
>   additional 5% off orders over $75.
>   **Guarantee:** Products may be returned if
>   still brand new so they can be resold
>   (PACK VERY WELL WHEN RE-
>   TURNING PRODUCTS).

Encyclopedia Britannica
310 South Michigan Ave.
Chicago, IL 60604
Phone: 800-323-1229
>   Check on year end specials when new
>   year's edition is released. As of April,
>   1995, '94 Britannica's were selling for
> $1299.00, a $300 savings. Availability
>   dependent on stock on hand. Also
>   publishes The Annals of America.

Eric Kline Books
established 1985
Marketing Director
P.O. Box 829
Santa Monica, CA 90404
Phone: 310-395-8825

Adult catalog, store and book club
>   Out of print and rare books. Art-architec-
>   ture, Judaica, German language, leather-
>   bound sets.
>   **Discount:** 10% to 20% trade.

Farm Country General Store
established 1991
95% home schoolers
Larry G. Schertz
Rte. 1 Box 63
Metamora, IL 61548
Phone: 309-367-2844
>   800-551-3276 (orders only)
Fax: 309-367-2844
Christian catalog
>   General education. Nutrition, health,
>   toys, games, K-12 educational materials,
>   all subjects. Annual catalog.
>   **Discount:** Majority of products are sold
>   at discount, in the range of 10-20%.
>   **Guarantee:** 30 day return policy if
>   returned in resalable condition.

Fireside Classics
established 1994
Tami Whitmore
17 Berk Road
Roosevelt, WA 99356
Phone: 509-896-2911
Fax: 509-837-6223
Christian catalog
>   Classic books, classic audio books,
>   classic video books for the whole family.
>   Age group: K-Adult.
>   **Discount:** 10% discount on all orders.
>   Free shipping on orders over $100.
>   Catalog available to all for free. All
>   orders will be filled within 30 days.

For the Love of Learning
established 1993
90% home schoolers
Caroline Penner
9638 73 Ave.
Edmonton, AB T6E 1B2 Canada
Phone: 403-431-2861
Christian all-inclusive catalog; book parties
> PreK-9, all subjects. Games, foreign languages, dictionaries, Usborne books, eyewitness books.
> **Discount:** Generally sell at 10% discount off suggested retail price. Some exceptions, but not many.
> **Guarantee:** Items, except cassettes, may be returned for refund within 30 days in resalable condition less shipping charges.

Foundation for American Christian Education (F.A.C.E.)
established 1965
George Brown, Executive Director
PO Box 9444
Chesapeake, VA 23321-9444
Phone: 804-488-6601
Fax: 804-488-5593
Christian nonsectarian specialty catalog
> F.A.C.E. Family Catalog, K-Adult/ biannual, no charge. Catalog focus: Christian history, literature, Principle Approach helps. Original 1828 Noah Webster dictionary.
> **Discount:** Sells at discount. Member prices, wholesale prices and extra discounts for teachers, students and clergy. Small membership fee. Members get substantial discounts and other educational benefits.

Free Spirit Publishing
established 1983
Cynthia Cain
400 First Ave. North, #616
Minneapolis, MN 55401
Phone: 800-735-7323
Fax: 612-337-5050
All-inclusive catalog
> FREE SPIRIT PUBLISHING, SELF-HELP FOR KIDS catalog distributed 3x/ year. Catalog focus: self-help for kids; learning and life skills for children, teens, teachers and parents.
> **Discount:** 10-24 products = 10% discount; 25-49 products = 15% discount; 50-99 products = 20% discount; 100+ products = 25% discount
> **Guarantee:** If anything you receive does not meet with your full approval, we will make it up by exchange, credit, or a refund.

Garden of Dreams
established 1990
75% home schoolers
Kimberli Swann, Owner
3442 N.W. 32 Court
Lauderdale Lakes, FL 33309
Phone: 305-733-9828
All-inclusive catalog
> GARDEN OF DREAMS annual catalog; age group: 2-adult; hard cover books sold at discount. Focus: Quality books, musical instruments, arts & crafts, science & nature materials, audio and video, gifts.
> **Discount:** 10% off list price on hard cover books every day. Monthly specials. Special orders welcomed.
> **Guarantee:** 100% satisfaction.

Gentle Wind, a
established 1981
20% home schoolers
Jill Person, President
P.O. Box 3103
Albany, NY 12203
Phone: 518-436-0391
Catalog
> Children's audio, storytelling, music,
> PreK through 12 years old.
> **Discount:** 10% catalog discount.
> **Guarantee:** Defective tapes replaced at
> no charge - but accidents can happen,
> especially when children are involved.
> We will replace any damaged tape if you
> send us the broken shell and $3.00 to
> cover postage and handling.

God's World Books
established 1943
30% home schoolers
Stephen Lutz, Manager
P.O. Box 2330
Asheville, NC 28802
Phone: 704-253-8063
Fax: 704-253-1556
Christian catalog
> GOD'S WORLD BOOKS catalog. 14
> major catalogs mailed yearly; divided
> into 2 tracks: 5 catalogs to parents and
> home schoolers and 9 catalogs mailed to
> Christian school teachers for classroom
> orders. Books are for K-8th graders,
> come from both Christian and secular
> publishers, and are screened for educa-
> tional, aesthetic, and moral value. Free
> catalogs. Call 1-800-951-2665. No
> obligation.
> **Discount:** All books sold in sets are
> discounted; some individual books are
> discounted as well.
> **Guarantee:** 100% money-back guaran-
> tee on all products.

Good Impressions Rubber Stamps
established 1981
Dale Michels
P.O. Box 33
Shirley, WV 26434
Phone: 304-758-4252
Fax: 304-758-4431
Catalog
> Rubber stamps with Victorian and arche-
> typal images. All ages.
> **Discount:** Unmounted stamps at 50%.
> **Guarantee:** Satisfaction.

Gospel Mission
established 1975
Marketing Director — Retail Sales
Box 318
Choteau, MT 59422
Phone: 406-466-2311
Fax: 406-466-2311
Christian catalog
> Wholesale Christian book outlet. Free
> catalog.
> **Discount:** 30%-60% off retail.

Gourmet Guides
established 1973
Jean Bullock
Pier 12, Sandy Beach Road
Vallejo, CA 94590
Phone: 707-644-6872
Fax: 707-554-1234
Specialty catalog and book club for adults
> Gourmet Guides issues a free monthly
> catalog of bargain cookbooks of interest
> to professional chefs, collectors and
> serious cooks.
> **Discount:** All books priced at 40% to
> 90% discount.
> **Guarantee:** Return in 2 weeks for full
> refund.

Graphic Design Book Club
Jim Walding, Marketing Director
1507 Dana Avenue
Cincinnati, OH 45207
Phone: 513-531-2222
Fax: 513-531-4744
Adult book club

Books for graphic design and production professionals to help them work smarter, faster, more creatively, and more profitably. After purchasing book through the joining offer, members are required to purchase one additional book in the next six months.

Discount: Members save 15%-20% on each book they purchase, and up to 65% on special sales.

Guarantee: Members may return any book for full refund or credit.

Great Christian Books
established 1970
Dean Andreola, Director of Marketing
229 South Bridge St.
P.O. Box 8000
Elkton, MD 21922-8000
Phone: 800-569-2481; 410-392-0800
Fax: 410-392-3103
Christian catalog and store

Age group: children and adults. 13,000 Christian books, Bibles, music, records and cassettes of interest to home schoolers at discount prices.

Discount: GCB "discounts whatever we can to save you money. We may on occasion offer free shipping on select products. We will 'match or beat' any competitor's published price (some restrictions apply—policy applies to items under $100 retail)."

Dues: $5.00, to receive all 12 catalogs. Canada/Mexico dues: $8.00. Overseas dues: $12.00. No obligation to buy.

Guarantee: No fuss guarantee. If you are not satisfied for any reason, GCB will promptly and cheerfully exchange, refund or credit. Returns must be made within 30 days of purchase with copy of invoice.

Heppner & Heppner Construction
established 1993
80% home schoolers
Miriam Heppner
Box 7
109 Wabasha
Warroad, MN 56763
Phone: 800-257-1994; 218-386-1994
Christian catalog and store

Christian bookstore and gift shop with home school educational materials. K-12 educational catalog.

Discount: $100 or more qualifies for 10% discount on a regular basis. Some selected titles are offered below retail.

HIS Publishing Co.
established 1988
Jack & Vicky Goodchild
1732 NE Third Ave.
Ft. Lauderdale, FL 33305
Phone: 305-764-4567
Christian all-inclusive specialty catalog

Supplying home educators with creative unit study programs plus quality materials for the four R's: reading, writing, 'rithmetc and reference resources. Specializing in Konos curriculum. K-12 catalog with some adult titles.

Discount: Volume discounts: Over $100 = 5%; over $150 = 10% on all products excluding Konos.

Guarantee: All merchandise can be returned within 30 days if in resalable condition.

History Book Club Inc.
established 1947
Nancy R. M. Whitin, Director
Time & Life Building
1271 Avenue of the Americas
New York, NY 10020
Phone: 212-522-1212
Fax: 212-522-0303
Adult book club
    History books for the educated layman,
    from ancient history to military history to
    current affairs.

Home Bound Books
established 1993
80% home schoolers
Val Houlihan
2141 N. 7th Road
Huntley, MT 59037
Phone: 406-348-2585
Christian all-inclusive catalog and store
    K-12, all educational products. Curricu-
    lum and supplements.
    Discount: Generally 10% off suggested
    retail.

Home Computer Market
established 1993
Tammy or Dan Kihlstadius, Owners
PO Box 385377
Bloomington, MN 55438
Phone: 612-844-0462
Fax: 612-831-0462
E-mail: aol: The Market
Christian specialty catalog
    Catalog targets ages 2-18. Sells educa-
    tional software, computer hardware and
    related book titles.
    Discount: "Our listed prices are dis-
    counted 20-35% off retail on almost all of
    our books and software!"
    Guarantee: Almost all software is
    satisfaction guaranteed.

Home Education Press
established 1983
90% home schoolers
Mark and Helen Hegener
P.O. Box 1083
1814 Hwy. 20 E.
Tonasket, WA 98855
Phone: 509-486-1351
Fax: 509-486-2628
E-mail: Hegener@aol.com
All-inclusive catalog
    Home Education Press Catalog targeted
    to parents. Catalog focus: books and
    special publications, HEM & back issues.
    Publisher of GOOD STUFF: LEARN-
    ING TOOLS FOR ALL AGES and
    ALTERNATIVES IN EDUCATION.
    HEM has a base rate of $24/year but is
    offered to families for $20.00. Single
    issue regularly $4.50; to families $3.50.
    Discount: Home school support groups
    can purchase at wholesale rates or just 2-
    3 families ordering together.

Home School Supply House
Shelli and Bruce Owen, Partners
P.O. Box 2000
280 West Center
Beaver, UT 84713
Phone: 801-438-1254
All-inclusive catalog
    Pre-K through high school, all subjects.
    Targets home schoolers. Uses cost in
    relation to quality in making selections
    (i.e. paperbacks over hardcovers of same
    title). Limited computer software. Vid-
    eos, if price is fair for content.
    Discount: 10 books with study guide for
    each reading level - 10% discount. 12+
    books - 10% discount from our Book-
    shelf Reading Program. 5% discount on
    shipping for orders over $100.00 Janu-
    ary-March of each year. Additional
    discounts available for people represent-

ing our company at shows or for a group. They must call for more information.
Guarantee: Books returned in new condition - full refund up to 30 days - after that credit with store for other items.

Home Works, the
established 1992
95% home schoolers
Paula Marquis
1760 Groves Road
RR #2
Russell, ON K4R 1E5 Canada
Phone: 613-445-3142
Fax: 613-445-0587
Christian catalog
Annual catalog of home schooling materials with emphasis on Canadian materials, speaking, consulting. Age group targeted: Preschool to secondary, plus family books. Catalog focus: Canadian home school needs.
Discount: Some quantity discounts available.
Guarantee: 15 days to look over materials. Complete money-back if returned resalable.

Homeschool Associates
established 1988
100% home schoolers
Steve Moitozo, Executive Director
116 Third Avenue
Auburn, ME   04210
Phone: 207-777-1700   800-882-2828
Fax: 207-777-1776
Store
Has 20,000 volume Used Curriculum Store for walk-ins and mail order. Toll free 800-882-2828 (certain states), others call 207-777-1700. Buys used textbooks. Outfits Homeschoolers' Bookmobile. Savings relative to condition of books and demand for titles. Query for more information.

Homeschool Seller
established 1993
David Orth, Marketing Director — Retail Sales
PO Box 19 Dept. HLI
Cherry Valley, MA 01611-3148
Phone: 508-791-8332
Fax: 508-791-8165
Christian catalog
Used curriculum listings catalog, published 9X per year. Anyone can list for free and then pay a 15% commission when their materials sell. We operate on the "honor system", which has, so far, worked quite well. One year subscription (9 issues) is $7.00.

Homeschooling Book Club
50% home schoolers
Sharon Peterson, Director of Marketing
1000 E. Huron
Milford, MI 48381
Phone: 810-685-8773
Fax: 810-685-8776
Christian catalog
K-12, all educational subjects.
Discount: Generally provide a 20% to 50% discount. Query.

Hometext Inc.
established 1993
100% home schoolers
Gail Hissins
283 Nevins Street
Brooklyn, NY 11217
Phone: 718-852-6583
Christian all-inclusive catalog
Supplier of new and reconditioned (used) books of all publishers, both religious and secular, from a single source. Age group targeted: 5-20. Catalog focus: school books. Distributes to all major publishers in all subject areas.
Discount: Sells at discount.

Hotho & Co.
established 1961
Donna Hotho, President
Box 9738
Ft. Worth, TX 76147-2738
Phone: 817-335-1833
Fax: 817-335-2300
Children and adult catalog
 Art books, cookbooks, reference, biographies, literature, no textbooks.
 Discount: Discounts vary. Suggest you call or write for a catalog.
 Guarantee: 100% guarantee, 30 day return policy.

Jewish Publication Society
established 1888
Donna Weber, Director, Marketing
600 Sanders St.
Scranton, PA 18505 (UPS)
1930 Chestnut St.
Philadelphia, PA 19103
Phone: 215-564-5925 800-334-3151
Fax: 215-564-6640
Catalog and book club
 Jewish books for secular and Jewish readers; children and adults. Call for free catalog.

JUBILEE! Curriculum Shopper (store name: Educational A+dvantage)
Terry McGee
2709 Highland Ave.
Montgomery, AL 36107
Phone: 205-834-6374
Christian nonsectarian catalog and store
 New products at discount for unit study users and those seeking to enhance their PreK-12 curriculum. Catalog design makes it easy to find a specific type of book. Home educators, teachers and parents will find it an excellent source for informative and fun books, games and kits that meet educational objectives children need. Children and adults can learn together. Guaranteed lowest discount prices on everything (except some publishers' restrictions). We have established catalog prices, but will match any competitor's regular catalog price (not specials) if your order includes: 1) the name of the company, 2) the current catalog issue number, 3) price they have listed. Also, if you find a lower price within 30 days of your order, we will refund the price difference if you write and include a copy of your order and the above information. Please send $2 p&h, $3 refunded on your first order. Catalog free at home school curriculum fairs.
 Guarantee: 30-day, full money-back guarantee for any unused product (postage excluded), except audio and video tapes which will be replaced only if damaged. Guaranteed replacement for damaged products.

Judaica Book Catalogue
established 1948
Fiorella de Lima, Editor
68-22 Eliot Avenue
Middle Village, NY 11379
Phone: 718-456-8611
Fax: 718-894-2818
Judaica Catalog and book club
 A catalogue of popular Judaic books is issued twice a year. Also have language cassette tapes and videos for children. A fine collection of Judaical books for young readers. All age groups. Contact Marvin Sekler for special sales. Books are sold on a non-return basis. This ensures low prices.

Kidtec
established 1994
100% home schoolers
Melanie Cornell
PO Box 5431
23629 Fagerlie Rd. 95602 (UPS)
Auburn, CA 95603
Phone: 916-268-8454; 800-884-8454
Fax: 916-268-3645
Christian catalog
    Educational Software for home
    schoolers; 18 months to adult.
    Discount: 30% average discounts - some
    even more! Just ask.
    Guarantee: Satisfaction guaranteed.

Laissez Faire Book Club
Andrea Rich, President
938 Howard St., Ste. 202
San Francisco, CA 94103
Phone: 415-541-9780   800-326-0996
Fax: 415-541-0597
E-mail: LFB@Panix.com
Catalog and book club
    Books, tapes on free market economics,
    libertarian thought, current issues. Prima-
    rily adults, but some books for children,
    5-15 years of age.
    Discount: In-bulk discounts are given.
    Book club members are given 10% off all
    prices, even those already on sale.
    Guarantee: 30 days.

Latter Day Family Resources
established 1989
Rick Hopkins, Proprietor
140 N. Main St.
Spanish Fork, UT 84660
Phone: 801-798-2106 800-290-2283 (orders
only)
Fax: 801-798-2067
Christian catalog and store
    The Latter Day Family Newsletter pub-
    lished every other month. 2 catalogs/ 2X

year, spring and fall. K-12 all subjects.
Full home school curriculum offered.
Topics include teaching the Gospel
(LDS), good reading, home school helps,
parenting, language arts, history, love of
liberty, math, science, art, music, dance,
foreign language, thinking skills, life
skills, self-reliant living.
Discount: 10-40% on most products.
Guarantee: Full money-back guarantee
if not satisfied. Return in stiff box, if
resalable, full money back.

Laurelwood Publications
Mark and Mary Ellen Tedrow
Route 1 Box 878
Bluemont, VA 22012
Phone: 703-554-2500 (M-F 1-5 p.m. EST)
Fax: 703-554-2938
Christian all-inclusive catalog
    New curriculum at discount prices, all
    subject areas, preK-12, Christian as well
    as secular products. Used curriculum
    taken on consignment for resale to
    schools and home schoolers.
    Discount: New product discounts range
    from 5%. Discount increases with
    quantity purchased. Used curriculum:
    savings from 25% to 75%.

Learning Lights
(formerly Covenant Christian Services)
established 1990
95% home schoolers
Vickie and Warren Jensen
PO Box 40875
85 Azalea Drive
Eugene, OR 97404
Phone: 503-689-5258
Christian all-inclusive catalog
    Formerly Covenant Christian Services.
    1st - 9th grade, expanding to preschool
    and high school. Non-text teaching/
    learning materials, math manipulatives

Learning Lights—continued

and supplements, science kits, games, multi-grade materials, Bible studies, language arts (phonics, grammar, composition, literature resource, handwriting), social studies, history helps, geography reproducibles, art workbooks and supplies. Sells products that are secular and Christian and/or secular by Christian writers.

Discount: Approximately 10% on nearly all products. Some products discounted 15%-20%.

Guarantee: 30 days in salable condition - request authorization to return or exchange item before.

Library & Educational Services
established 1983
Dick Proctor
PO Box 146
Berrien Springs, MI 49103
Phone: 616-471-1400
Fax: 616-473-7323
Catalog

Sells only to home schoolers, libraries, churches, and schools. PreK through adult level materials, including literature and educational items. No textbooks, but strong in supplemental education.

Discount: Minimum 30% discount and some products up to 80% off retail.

Guarantee: 30 day return policy.

Lifetime Books & Gifts
established 1987
90% home schoolers
Bob and Tina Farewell, Buyers
3900 Chalet Suzanne Drive
Lake Wales, FL 33853-7763
Phone: 813-676-6311; 800-377-0390
Fax: 813-676-2732

Christian catalog

THE ALWAYS INCOMPLETE RESOURCE GUIDE AND CATALOG published annually with updates. Age group targeted: birth to adult. For families that home educate their children - also for Christian and private school resource for library.

Discount: 5 or more per title: 5% off. 10 or more per title: 10% off.

Little Dania's Juvenile Promotions
established 1978
Phil Hochberg, President
100 Paterson Plank Road
Jersey City, NJ 07307
Phone: 201-659-2317; 718-782-0405
Fax: 201-659-3631
Catalog in progress

Juvenile promotions, reprints & remainders. Warehouse: 2500 titles.

Discount: 50% discount.

Little Schoolhouse
established 1989
Cathy Bigsby
PO Box 88
Lawtey, FL 32058
Phone: 904-782-1144
Christian catalog and store

Sells retail and discount, K-12 Christian materials, both new and used teaching curriculum. Includes some secular.

Discount: New products receive an approximate 10-20% off cover price; used products are sold at approximately 40-75% off cover price.

Maranatha Publications Inc.
established 1979
Gerrie Weiner, Asst. Director
PO Box 1799
Gainesville, FL 32602

Phone: 904-375-6000
Fax: 904-335-0080
<u>Children and adult specialty Christian publisher</u>
>   Story of Liberty - Charles C. Coffin;
>   Study Guide Story of Liberty - Steve C.
>   Dawson; Sweet Land Liberty - Charles C.
>   Coffin. 8 years through adult.
>   **Discount:** 10 - 19 copies = 5%; 20 - 29
>   copies = 10%; 30 - 39 copies = 15%

Miserly Moms
established 1994
Beau & Jonni McCoy
P.O. Box 32174
San Jose, CA 95152
E-mail: Miserly Mom (America On Line address)
<u>All-inclusive specialty book</u>
>   Guidebook for living on one income in a
>   two-income economy. Practical tips to
>   save big on groceries, babies, medical,
>   etc. Family management, finances, home
>   management.
>   **Discount:** 10% for group purchases over
>   10 books.
>   **Guarantee:** Full purchase refund if
>   unsatisfied.

Mountain View Books
established 1990
90% home schoolers
Judy Addington, Owner
Route 1 Box 1020
Elizabethton, TN 37643
Phone: 615-542-3374 (orders)
<u>Christian catalog and store</u>
>   Functions: through mail order, book
>   fairs, and store. Targets all ages. Catalog
>   focus: mostly home schoolers.
>   **Discount:** Sells some items at discount.
>   Contact them for discount information.

Music Stand®
1 Music Stand Plaza
66 Benning St.
W. Lebanon, NH 03784-3400
Phone: 800-717-7010; 800-414-4010 (Customer Service)
Catalog and Store
>   Music and music-related items: totes,
>   mugs, jewelry and more.
>   **Discount:** Join ACCOP (lifetime membership costs $20). If you join when
>   placing your first order you can deduct
>   10% from your first order, and receive
>   10% Savings on future Music Stand
>   Merchandise. Group Sales available for
>   fund raising, award programs, group
>   purchases and special occasions. Call and
>   ask for Group Service Manager.
>   **Guarantee:** If for any reason you are not
>   completely satisfied, item can returned.
>   They will refund, credit or replace the
>   item....whichever you prefer.

North Light Book Club
Jim Walding, Marketing Director
3637 Woodburn Ave (UPS)
1507 Dana Ave
OH 45207
Phone: 513-531-2222
Fax: 513-531-4744
<u>Adult book club</u>
>   Hundreds of art instruction books and
>   videos to help artists at all skill levels
>   improve or discover new techniques.
>   **Discount:** Members save 15% to 20%
>   on each book they purchase, and up to
>   65% on special sales. You must purchase
>   books through the joining offer, then you
>   are under no obligation to make additional purchases.
>   **Guarantee:** Members may return any
>   book for a full refund or credit.

Parsonage Books
established 1984
Deborah Marsh
PO Box 388
132 E. Broadway St.
Brook, IN 47922
Phone: 219-275-6553
Christian catalog

K-12, all subjects with a unit study approach. Products carried have been tested by Parsonage's tutoring students and their own children. Selection is designed to help the student master the material, not to confine him to grade level busy work. Catalog features Christian and quality secular materials to meet Parsonage's goals from a unit study approach.

Discount: 10% discounts on some items. Additional discounts plus free shipping are offered at conventions.

Guarantee: 100% satisfaction or you may return the material for a full refund of the purchase price. The materials must be in salable condition and returned within 6 months of purchase.

Pilgrim Publishers
established 1983
50+% home schoolers
Stanley K. or Janice E. Brubaker
22777 State Road #119
Goshen, IN 46526
Phone: 219-534-2245
Fax: 219-534-2333
Christian catalog

NATURE'S WORKSHOP 64-page catalog, nature-related items, coloring book, stationery, science equipment, arts, crafts, books, field guides. Christian based but doesn't exclude secular products but might include a sheet to site objectionable passages for Christians.

For preschool-high school and adult.
Discount: Up to 10% discounts on orders of 5 or more on some items and categories. Query for further discount terms.
Guarantee: Purchase price refunded on any item returned within 60 days in resalable condition.

Play and Learn
established 1974
10-15% home schoolers
Ernie Meili
244 1st Ave. N.
Saskatoon, SK S7K 1X1 Canada
Phone: 306-934-0860
Fax: 306-934-0857
All-inclusive catalog and store

Learning games, manipulatives, teaching aides, motivational materials, bulletin board materials, workbooks and idea books for all subjects, primarily grades K-9. All inclusive, with some Christian products.

Discount: Discount card: for each 10 purchases customer receives 10% off accumulated value of the ten purchases to use as credit for additional purchases in the store. For institutions: open 10% discount on all products, except furniture.

Guarantee: Books are nonreturnable, but other products are returnable within two weeks, manufacturer's warranty honored.

Rainbow Re-source Center
established 1989
100% home schoolers
Bob and Linda Schneider
8227 Ulah Road
Cambridge, IL 61238
Phone: 309-937-3385

Catalog
Sells new educational materials, resells used educational materials. RAINBOW RE-PORTER (used books). RAINBOW RE-SOURCE CENTER CATALOG: New and Reviewed Products. General home school products.
Discount: Most prices in our catalog are lower than suggested list price.
Guarantee: 100% refund on cost of book returned in salable condition.

Relaxed Home Schooler / Ambleside
Educational Press
established 1990
100% home schoolers
Mary Hood
PO Box 2524
Cartersville, GA 30120
Phone: 404-917-9141
Christian all-inclusive catalog
THE RELAXED HOME SCHOOL SHOPPER Catalog published quarterly.
Discount: Sometimes sells at discount.

Roots & Wings Educational Catalog
established 1989
10% home schoolers
Anne Wilson
P.O. Box 3348
Boulder, CO 80307
Phone: 303-494-1833   800-833-1787
Fax: 303-494-2693
All-inclusive catalog
Educational K-6th grade. Multicultural, Australia, peace, ecology, special needs, inclusion, parenting and families.
Discount: $200-$499 = 2 1/2%; $500-$999 = 5%; $1,000-$1,999 = 10%; Over $2,000 = 10% plus free shipping.
Guarantee: Unconditional guarantee that customer is satisfied.

Scholar's Bookshelf
established 1975
Rose Ward, Marketing Director — Retail Sales
110 Melrich Rd.
Cranbury, NJ 08512
Phone: 609-395-6933
Fax: 609-395-0755
Catalog
Contents include: history, literature, fine arts; music, social and political studies, psychology, philosophy, religion, Judaica, science, reference. Although all books are not discounted they do run sales with savings advertised up to 75%. One of their catalogs consisted of fine arts books including: general works, reference, Greece, Rome & the Ancient World, Medieval art, printed books and manuscripts, the Renaissance, and a special bargain section listing books under $5.00.
Minimum $10.00 prepaid or $15.00 credit card order for individuals.
Guarantee: Can be returned for full credit if received within 30 days.

Scholars' Books Inc.
established 1985
Shiaw Lin, President
1379 E. 53rd St.
Chicago, IL 60615
Phone: 312-288-6565
Fax: 312-268-9854
Adult book club

Scholastic Book Clubs, Inc.
PO Box 7500
2931 East McCarty Street
Jefferson City, MO 65102
Phone: 314—636-5271; 800-724-2424
Children's book club
Scholastic Book Clubs sell to schools and home schools only. Club Names include:

Scholastic Book Clubs, Inc.—continued

Firefly Book Club is preschool book club.

SeeSaw Book Club is Kindergarten through first grade.

Lucky Book Club is 2nd and 3rd grade.

Arrow Book Club is 4th, 5th and 6th.

TAB Book Club is 7th - 9th and up.

Cynthia Maloney, 212-343-4628, general # 343-6100, ask for book club marketing director. $10.00 minimum order or ten paid items.

Discount: All books are discounted.

Guarantee: 14-21 day return option.

Shekinah Curriculum Cellar
established 1988
W. Kent & Michele Robinson
1260 Logan Ave. Suite A-5
Costa Mesa, CA 92626
Phone: 714-751-7767 (outgoing message only)
Fax: 714-751-7725
Christian catalog

All subjects, all grade levels. Lowest price guarantee - we match any current low price from any other source. Send $1.00 for catalog. Catalogs are provided free of charge to groups. Just send us your group's name, address and current membership, and we will send catalogs.

Discount: Some of our products are discounted.

Guarantee: Satisfaction guaranteed or your money back.

Small Ventures
established 1987
95% home schoolers
Bonnie L. Dettmer
11023 Watterson Drive
Dallas, TX 75228

Phone: 214-681-1728
Fax: 214-681-0139
Christian catalog

Pre-K through adult, all subject areas. Concentration in phonics and history.

Discount: Discounts as indicated in catalog.

Guarantee: 30 day return policy in salable condition.

Sonlight Curriculum Ltd.
established 1990
100% home schoolers
John and Sarita Holzmann
8185 South Grant Way
Littleton, CO 80122
Phone: 303-730-6292
Fax: 303-795-8668
E-mail: #75521, 2364
Christian all-inclusive specialty catalog

Emphasis is on international literature-based historically-oriented materials for all age levels. K-8, all subjects.

Discount: Sliding discounts on package purchases range from 2% to 7% discount. All purchases over $100 receive 10% discount over and above the sliding scale discount. $2.00 for the catalog which is refunded with first purchase.

Guarantee: 30-day full money back guarantee (less shipping).

Still Waters Revival Books
established 1985
85% home schoolers
Reg Barrow
4710-37A Ave.
Edmonton, AB T6L 3T5 Canada
Phone: 403-450-3730
Christian catalog

Primarily Christian religious titles sold at discount (i.e. Christian Reconstruction and Reformation resources) with a few pages devoted to "how-to" home school titles. Free catalog upon request - all mail order including rare and hard to find items.

Story House Corporation

Marketing Director — Retail Sales
Bindery Lane
Charlotteville, NY 12036
Phone: 800-847-2105
Fax: 607-397-8282
Catalog

Sells prebound paperbacks to schools and individuals outside New York state. Individuals must place order with check or a major credit card (Visa & Master Card).

Strand Bookstore

Marketing Director — Retail Sales
828 Broadway
New York, NY 10003
Phone: 212-473-1452
Fax: 212-473-2591
Catalog and store

Strand is the world's largest used bookstore with over 2.5 million books on 8 miles of shelving. A must visit for book lovers, most of these books are priced at 20-80% off the list price, with tens of thousands of reviewer's copies at 50% off the publisher's list price and an enormous stock of quality remainders. We also house a fine collection of rare, unusual, and first edition titles in our Rare Book Department. We sell hardback books by the foot starting at $10.00 a foot with decorative books at higher prices. We have a large suggestion of used Britannicas. Write, call, or fax us for our free "specials" catalog. Membership in Antiquarian Bookseller Association.

Discount: Most books are priced at 20-80% off the list price. Tens of thousands of reviewer's copies at 50% off the publisher's list price.
Guarantee: Satisfaction guaranteed or your money back.

T & D Christian Sales

established 1977
Tim Todd, Marketing Director — Retail Sales
PO Box 4140
Cleveland, TN 37320
Phone: 800-423-9595; 615-476-8571
Fax: 615-472-4510
Catalog

Discount source for Christian books & Bibles. Catalog contents include: sermon outline sets; compubible; music; products from: Kregel, Baker Book House, Bethany/Scripture Press, Revell, Wm. B. Eerdman's, Moody Press; Zandervan; Bible and church history; discount Bibles; Bible reference; Christian living; commentaries; Biblical theology; expository sermon helps; Greek/Hebrew reference; Christian library classics; inspiration; bargain pacs; for the children. Returns are permitted only if T&D shipped the wrong book or if the book is defective or damaged in shipping. Any other reason will require a re-stock fee.

Thomas More Book Club

established 1939
Julie Bridge, Editor
205 W. Monroe St., 6th Flr.
Chicago, IL 60606
Phone: 312-609-8880   800-835-8965
Fax: 312-609-8891
Adult Catholic book club

Thomas More Book Club is a reading plan for adult Catholics. No obligation,

Thomas More Book Club—continued
newsletter mailed twelve times per year.
One main selection offered at a discount.
Also includes "Best of the New" list of
current books, videos and audios. List of
bargain books accompanies each mailing,
also. No pre-payment, no minimum
purchase.
Discount: Main selection - current title -
offered at 20% off or more to members.
Bargain books available each month,
also. No obligation. Call 1-800-835-
8965 to enroll.
Guarantee: Members may return books
for a full refund within 30 days of purchase. Return postage paid. Videos and
audios may be returned for exchange if
defective.

Timberdoodle Company
established 1985
95% home schoolers
Deb and Dan Deffinbaugh
E. 1510 Spencer Lake Road
Shelton, WA 98584
Phone: 206-426-0672; 8:00 am. to 12 noon
Monday-Thursday
Fax: 206-427-5625
Catalog
    Biannual+ catalog (95% home
    schoolers). Ages 18 months-adult. "Our
    main area of emphasis is hands-on
    educational tools. We attempt to carry in
    our catalog things that are not readily
    available in local shops, particularly
    those items that enable the child to see
    and understand by doing." Subjects
    include: foreign languages, thinking
    skills, math manipulatives, math support
    materials, geography, science, creation
    science, art, physical fun, reading, lauri,
    parent's library, home business & fi-
    nances, music, sign language.

Discount: Retail sales only, up to 40%.
Guarantee: 60 day satisfaction, if
returned in resalable condition.

Time Warner Viewer's Edge
Lee Anderson
P.O. Box 3925
Milford, CT 06460
Phone: 800-224-9944; 203-876-9864; 212-
522-5183
Fax: 203-876-8234
E-mail: Compuserve: "Go:Vid"
Catalog
    Viewer's Edge advertises "the best video
    values anywhere. Guaranteed." Catalog
    includes: screen classics, comedy, TV
    mini-series, family fun, cult classics, TV
    drama, movie musicals, adult only, travel
    videos, and more.
Guarantee: Their guarantee: "If you
find a lower price for any tape you
purchase, just let us know. We'll refund
the difference ... plus 10%!" If you're
not completely satisfied, you may exchange an item or request a refund - no
questions asked.

Titus Woman's Homeschool Potpourri
established 1990
90% home schoolers
Jenny Sockey
220 State Street South
Kirkland, WA 98033
Phone: 206-822-7337
Fax: 206-803-0495
Christian store
    75% are used books, Christian curricu-
    lum, 25% are new. Discount on new
    given as well. Prefer current editions.
    Home school related books, toys and
    games. Do sell nationwide by phone
    orders. No catalog available.

Usborne Books-Consultant Services
Kathy Plecinski
Marketing Director — Retail Sales
Div. of Educational Development Corp.
PO Box 470663
Tulsa, OK 74147
Phone: 800-475-4522
Fax: 800-747-4509
Book parties
   An individual can host a home book
   party. Compensation for hosting the
   party results in free merchandise, based
   on the retail sale amount of books sold on
   a per party basis. Customer specials
   offered. Other incentives, contact
   Usborne for more information.
   Guarantee: 30 day guarantee and 1/2
   price replacement on damaged books
   after 30 days.

Veritas Book Club, The
established 1954
Roger Corbin, Manager
6 N. Water St.
Greenwich, CT 06830
Phone: 203-531-7755
Adult book club
   Books relating to the conservative move-
   ment in America, the new right politics
   and the history of conservatism. Must
   purchase three books to become a Veritas
   Book Club member.
   Discount: Quantity purchases sold at
   discount.
   Guarantee: Refund if not fully satisfied.

World Book Educational Products
101 NW Point Blvd.
Elk Grove Village, IL 60007
Phone: 800-621-8202
   Check on the possibility of year end
   savings when the new year's edition is
   released.

Woodworker's Book Club
Jim Walding, Marketing Director
3637 Woodburn Avenue (UPS)
1507 Dana Avenue
Cincinnati, OH 45207
Phone: 513-531-2222
Fax: 513-531-4744
Adult book club
   Books to help woodworkers perfect their
   skills and learn about new tools and
   techniques.
   Discount: Members save 15%-20% on
   each book they purchase, and up to 50%
   on special sales. Must purchase books
   per the joining offer, and are not required
   to purchase any additional books.
   Guarantee: May return any book for
   full refund or credit.

Writer's Digest Book Club
Jim Walding, Marketing Director
1507 Dana Avenue
Cincinnati, OH 45207
Phone: 513-531-2690
Fax: 513-531-4744
Adult book club
   Hundreds of writing instruction books to
   help writers at all skill levels hone their
   skills and sell their writing.
   Discount: Members save 15%-20% on
   every book they purchase, and up to 65%
   on special sales. You must purchase
   book per the joining offer, then purchase
   one book in the next six months.
   Guarantee: Members may return any
   book for a full refund or credit.

Young Writers Institute w/Sigmund Brouwer
established 1993
98% home schoolers
Debra Bell, Director
6 Royal Road
Palmyra, PA 17078

Phone: 717-838-6201
Fax: 717-838-6201
E-mail: DebraBell @ AOL.com
<u>Christian catalog</u>
Catalog: HOME SCHOOL RESOURCE CENTER "Resource for Creative Homeschooling". Age group: preschool

Young Writers Institute—continued
through high school. Specializes in children's literature, extensive list of historical fiction and language arts, but covers all disciplines.

Discount: On orders over $200, customers receive a 15% discount. Book rate shipping is a flat $3.50 regardless of the size of the order. For UPS shipping, add $5.00 to the $3.50.

Guarantee: 30-day money back guarantee if materials are returned in resalable condition.

Additional Source Information

BOOK LOOK
51 Maple Ave.
Warwick, NY 10990
Phone: 800-223-0540
FAX: 914-651-1233
Out-of-print search service. Cost as of April, 1995: $4.50 / month per title until book is located or until order is canceled.

ENCYCLOPEDIA OF ASSOCIATIONS
Gale Research
835 Penobscot Building
Detroit, MI 48226
Phone 800-877-4253
Source for locating associations consistent with one's own philosophy. Also lists book clubs.

LITERARY MARKET PLACE
R.R. Bowker
PO Box 31
New Providence, NJ 07974
Phone 908-464-6800; 800-521-8110
Extensive list of book clubs for children and adults.

Directory of
Resources
for
Stocking a Home Library
Conveniently

21st Century Education Resources
established 1990
95% home schoolers
Barbara Simkus
4248 Chicago Road
Warren, MI 48092
Phone: 810-978-9293
FAX: 810-978-2808
Christian catalog
   21st CENTURY EDUCATION RE-
   SOURCES, comprised of Blumenfeld
   and Charlotte Mason materials.

A Common Reader
James Mustich, Jr.
141 Tompkins Ave.
Pleasantville, NY 10570
Phone: 1-800-832-7323
FAX: 1-914-747-0778
Catalog for children and adults
   Subject areas from past catalogs include:
   Ancient Words, Permanent Library,
   Running in the Family, Featured Authors
   (including Jane Austin, the Brontes, C.S.
   Lewis and more), Humor, Holy Words,
   Books for Young Readers. Issued
   monthly.

A. W. Peller & Associates
established 1973
Carol Schweighardt
P.O. Box 106
Hawthorne, NJ 07507
Phone: 201-423-4666
FAX: 201-423-5569
All-inclusive specialty catalog
   BRIGHT IDEAS catalog focuses on
   gifted and talented, critical and creative
   thinking.

Alpha Plus
Janet R. Lathan
P.O. Box 185
Chewsville, MD 21721
Phone: 301-733-1456
Specialty catalog
   Mathematics oriented catalog.

Aquarian Agent Book Club
Henry Weingarten, Director
350 Lexington Ave., #402
New York, NY 10016
Phone: 212-949-7211
Adult book club

Atco School Supply
established 1989
90% home schoolers
Tammy R. Casado
425 East Sixth Street, Unit 105
Corona, CA 91719
Phone: 909-272-2926
Christian catalog and store
   K-12 catalog; all subject areas.

BACK PACK
established 1990
99% home schoolers
David and Joan Cowell
PO Box 125
3200 Old Brick Rd.
Vanceboro, NC 28586 (UPS)
Ernul, NC 28527
Phone: 919-637-5137
Fax: 919-244-1912
Catalog and store
   New (50%) and used (50%) K-12 educa-
   tional materials. Store is a mix of new
   and used. Catalog is all new, and prod-
   ucts are sold at retail. Also sell at confer-
   ences and bookfairs.

Back to Basics
established 1993
100% home schoolers
Joyce L. Coates
3717 Friday Avenue
Everett, WA 98201
Phone: 206-259-1826
Christian catalog
    K-12 catalog, all academic subjects.

Baptist Sunday School Committee
established 1920
95% home schoolers
Wayne Sewell, Promotions Director
4605 N. State Line Avenue
Texarkana, TX 75503-2928
Phone: 903-792-2783 800-264-2482
Fax: 903-792-8128
Christian catalog
    Annual catalog; age group K-12. Distrib-
    utes Alpha Omega and Saxon math
    curriculums.

Beautiful Feet Books
established 1984
Rea and Russ Berg, Owners
139 Main Street
Sandwich Village, MA 02563
Phone: 508-833-8626
Christian specialty catalog and store
    Catalog is targeted to all age levels with
    focus on a literature approach to teaching
    U.S., medieval, and ancient history.
    Includes biographical, historical and
    classic literature from a Christian per-
    spective, as well as literature for use in
    teaching a providential approach to
    history for most historical periods.
    Catalog cost, $1.00.

Bendt Family Ministries
established 1990
99% home schoolers

Valerie and Bruce Bendt
333 Rio Vista Court
Tampa, FL 33604
Phone: 813-238-3721
Christian specialty catalog
    Pre-K-12th grade catalog. Focus: unit
    study materials, Christian.

Best Picks
established 1994
100% home schoolers
Linda Trumbo
5903 Grove Ave.
Richmond, VA 23226
Phone: 804-288-6402
Fax: 804-288-7678
Christian catalog
    PreK through high school. Unit study
    focus, all-inclusive, literary Great Books
    focus, all subject areas. Primarily Chris-
    tian.

Birch Court Books, Inc.
established 1989
95% home schoolers
Julie Agen
N7137 County Hwy. C
Seymour, WI 54165
Christian catalog
    Educational books, curriculum, games;
    K-12, all education subjects, plus litera-
    ture. Primarily Christian with some
    secular. No packaged curriculum.

Books of Light
established 1975
Leslie Swanson
289 S. Main St., Ste. 205
Alpharetta, GA 30201
Phone: 404-664-4886 800-336-7769
Fax: 404-664-4974
Nonsectarian adult catalog and book club
    We carry books that promote thinking

Books of Light—continued
> and creativity such as personal and
> spiritual growth, fiction, health, religion,
> philosophy, science fiction and fantasy.

Brook Farm Books
established 1981
Donn Reed
P.O. Box 246
Bridgewater, ME 04735
All-inclusive catalog
> Catalog & Resource Guide — THE
> HOME SCHOOL SOURCE BOOK, now
> in its second edition, lists more than 3000
> items, sources, resources (many free) for
> home schoolers. No date has been set for
> the third edition (probably early 1996).
> All reviews are subjective and will be
> included at the author's discretion. "I
> make my biases clear to the readers,"
> says the author, "so they aren't misled."

Brown Sugar & Spice Book Service
5% home schoolers
Jacqueline Blake, Director of Marketing
8584 Whitehorn
Romulus, MI 48174
Phone: 313-729-0501
All-inclusive specialty catalog
> Catalog of multi-cultural children's
> literature and black history teaching
> supplies. Specialize in Afro-centric.

Canadian Home Education Resources
Brenda Baradoy
7 Stanley Crescent S.W.
Calgary, AB T2S 1G1 Canada
Phone: 403-243-9727
Christian catalog
> K-12, all educational materials, Christian
> with some secular.

Catholic Homeschooler's Exchange
established 1994
Kathleen Bell
9336 Twin Mt. Circle
San Diego, CA 92126
Phone: 619-549-3802
Catholic catalog
> The CHEERFUL CATALOG printed
> within the pages of Cheerful Cherub
> Magazine.

Child's Dream
Holly Johansen
2990 Linden Drive
Boulder, CO 80304
Phone: 303-442-0437
All-inclusive specialty catalog
> Crafts and play items, natural, sewing
> kits, doll-making supplies.

Children's Braille Book Club
established 1927
Diane Croft, Marketing Manger
88 Saint Stephen St.
Boston, MA 02115
Phone: 617-266-6160
Fax: 617-437-0456
Children's book club
> Children's print, Braille books, pre-
> school-3rd grade. Membership is free;
> books range from $4.95-$14.95. $100 for
> yearly subscription, if preferable.

Children's Small Press Collection
established 1986
5% home schoolers
Kathleen Baxter
719 N. Fourth Ave.
Ann Arbor, MI 48104
Phone: 800-221-8056
All-inclusive catalog
> Family Favorites Tabloid, complimen-
> tary, targets home school market. Carries
> materials from small publishers.

Chinaberry Book Service
2780 Via Orange Way, Ste. B
Spring Valley, CA 91978
Phone: 800-776-2242
Fax: 619-670-5203
All-inclusive catalog
    Books and other treasures for the entire
    family. Primarily literature, some tapes,
    videos and games.

Christian Family Resources
established 1979
85-90% home schoolers
Veda & Ron Bunch
PO Box 195
Kit Carson, CO 80825-0195
Phone: 719-962-3228
Christian all-inclusive catalog and store
    Christian K-12 catalog, all educational
    materials, kitchen appliances and grind-
    ers, long-term storage foods.

Christian Life Workshops
established 1981
Dick Hoffman
P.O. Box 2250
Gresham, OR 97030
Phone: 503-667-3942
Fax: 503-665-6637
Christian catalog
    HOME SCHOOL FAVORITES Catalog.
    Home and family business newsletter
    with book section.

Christian Schools International
established 1919
10% home schoolers
Lori Feenstra, Director of Marketing
3350 East Paris Avenue S.E.
Grand Rapids, MI 49512
Phone: 616-957-1070 Ext. 263
Fax: 616-957-5022
Christian catalog
    Annual catalog. Focus: educational

curriculum; only their own publications
are in catalog.

Colburn's
10% home schoolers
P.O. Box 2530
Billings, MT 59103
Phone: 406-245-2158; 800-548-7031
Catalog and store
    K-12 educational supplier, with access to
    educational furniture. Store locations in
    Denver, Albuquerque and other locations.
    Denver is the main office. Brad Larson,
    VP Sales & Marketing, PO Box 9348
    Denver, CO 80209 ; physical 999 S.
    Jason Street, Denver, CO 80223, 303-
    778-1220; 800-275-8700.

Creative Home Teaching
established 1992
95% home schoolers
Jill Denly, Owner
P.O. Box 152581
San Diego, CA 92195
Phone: 619-263-8633
Catalog
    Offers curriculum for home schoolers.
    Catalog contains detailed explanation of
    each product. Age group targeted: Pre-
    K-12.

Creative Learning Systems
established 1983
10% home schoolers
Cat Melvin
16510 Via Esprillo
San Diego, CA 92127
Phone: 619-675-7700; 800-458-2880
Fax: 519-675-7700
All-inclusive catalog
    Transtech Catalog. Includes software,
    CDs, construction kits and educational
    supplies for K-12, with some adult books
    on the subject of education.

Curriculum Corner
established 1991
99% home schoolers
Debra G. Shelly
3620 N. Salina
Wichita, KS 67204
Phone: 316-838-2268
Christian catalog and store
> K-12 Christian educational materials, all
> subjects.

Custom Curriculum Company
85% home schoolers
Ranell Curl
76504 Poplar St.
Oakridge, OR 97463
Phone: 503-782-2571
Fax: 503-782-2571
Christian catalog
> Distributes Bible, pre-school, math,
> language arts, science and history.

Eagle's Nest
established 1991
Michele Szabo
1539 Oakwood Drive
Escalon, CA 95320
Phone: 209-838-3193
Christian catalog and store
> K-12, all educational subjects.

Education PLUS+
Dr. Ronald Cannon, President
P.O. Box 1591
Sterling, VA 20167
Phone: 703-450-5326
Fax: 703-450-5326
Adult Christian catalog
> Education PLUS+ offers training materi-
> als designed by Ronald and Inge Cannon
> to assist parents/teachers in working with
> children and youth: interdisciplinary
> curriculum, biblical teaching methods,

recordkeeping and child development.
Materials also available which emphasize
parents mentoring their children into
adulthood, evaluating college, and exploring apprenticeship options. Free
catalog sent upon request.

Education Supply House
established 1991
Susan Winters
Route 1 Box 41
Martinsville, IL 62442
Phone: 217-382-4236
Christian all-inclusive catalog
> K-12 all education materials.

Elijah Company
established 1988
85% home schoolers
Chris Davis
Route 2 Box 100B
Crossville, TN 38555
Phone: 615-456-6284
Fax: 615-456-6384
Christian adult catalog
> Large annual catalog; biannual/supple-
> ments, all ages. Catalog focus: for
> parents, tailoring education to their
> family's needs and convictions.

Excellence in Education
established 1991
98% home schoolers
Carolyn or Martin Forte
527 Franklin Place
Monrovia, CA 91016
Phone: 818-357-4443
All-inclusive catalog
> K-adult. Focus: High interest/fun learn-
> ing materials; biographies for all reading
> levels.

Family Bookstores
20% home schoolers
Carolyn Wenzel
50 Route 46 E.
Mountain Lakes, NJ 07046
Phone: 800-695-2198
Christian catalog and store
Store with a catalog/resource list: sent on request. K-12 Christian religious and educational materials. One of a chain of 140 Christian bookstores. Home office is in Grand Rapids, MI.

Family Christian Academy
Robin and Ron Scarlata, Director of Marketing
487 Myatt Drive
Madison, TN 37115
Phone: 800-788-0840; 615-860-3000
Christian catalog and store
General catalog carries all K-12 educational material, some secular. Unit Study Catalog lists all unit studies. Will sell unit study program and ancillary books recommended in the unit study programs. Stores in 5415 "F" Kingston Pike, Knoxville, TN 37919, ph. 615-588-2106, and 487 Myatt Dr., Madison, TN 37115, ph. 615-860-3000.

Family Learning Center
Susan Simpson
Rt. 2 Box 264
Hawthorne, FL 32640
Phone: 904-475-3287
Christian catalog
Family Learning Center Catalog. Age group targeted: K-12 curriculum. Focus: Christian home school materials.

Family Learning Services
established 1991
95% home schoolers
Allan Ward
PO Box 9596
Birmingham, AL 35220
Phone: 205-854-6870
Fax: 205-856-6369
Adult catalog
Provide sound educational material, specifically common sense press products and reference materials. Age group targeted: Adults. Catalog focus: home schooling parents.

Family Legacy
David and Janice Price
8510 N. Knoxville, Ste. 152
Peoria, IL 61615
Phone: 309-243-7465; 800-207-7229
Fax: 309-693-2224
Catalog
Publishes Kidsco, a bible-based business curriculum for children. Resource guide.

Family Pastimes
established 1970
Jim Deacove
RR 4
Perth, ON K7H 3C6 Canada
Phone: 613-267-4819
Fax: 613-264-0696
All-inclusive specialty catalog
CO-OP GAMES Catalog: Sells a line of co-operative, educational games and books. All ages. Free catalog upon request. Has a recommended book list of other publishers' titles in their catalog.

Far Out Explorations
The Art Book Catalogue
Elaine Dimenstein
P.O. Box 308
Milford, CT 06460
Phone: 203-877-2962; 1-800-510-ARTS
Fax: 203-874-9099
Catalog
> Art books for preK through adults.
> Includes artists' biographies, how to look
> at art books, famous paintings books, art
> integrated into other subjects: math,
> science, history, multi-cultural, etc.

Fourth Corner Books
established 1993
98% home schoolers
John & Bernadine Rogstad
2132 Yew Street
Bellingham, WA 98226
Phone: 360-734-2204 (voice)
Fax: 360-676-8232
Christian catalog and store
> Catalog K-12, all subject areas, Christian
> as well as secular.

Gateway Curriculm Center
99% home schoolers
Vickey Smith
P.O. Box 280111
3952 Ronnie Ave. 38128
Memphis, TN 38168-0111
Phone: 901-382-6304
Christian store
> Small Christian store serving private and
> homeschoolers. Open part-time on
> Friday and Saturday afternoons only. No
> mail order.

genius tribe
established 1994
Grace Llewellyn
268 W. 7th
Eugene, OR 97401
Phone: 503-345-3358
Fax: 503-686-2315
All-inclusive catalog and store for children
and adults
> Focus: math, science, and other aca-
> demic areas, books on home schooling
> and alternative education, quality color-
> ing books, youth rights. Pre-K- adults.

God's Riches
established 1994
100% home schoolers
Debbie Rich
PO Box 560217
Miami, FL 33256-0217
phone: 305-667-3130 (voice mail)
Christian catalog
> K-12 Christian catalog, all subjects.

Greenleaf Press
established 1989
Rob Shearer
1570 Old Laguardo Road
Lebanon, TN 37087
Phone: 615-449-1617
Fax: 615-449-4018
Christian specialty catalog
> K-12, focus on history and nature study.

Happy Face School Supplies
established 1990
65% home schoolers
Kim Langlais
RR #1 Box 276A, Rte. #22
Petersburgh, NY 12138
Phone: 518-658-9409
Christian nonsectarian specialty catalog
> K-12 Christian catalog with emphasis on
> the young, featuring school supplies and

Christian gifts, with an emphasis on lower cost items. Catalog - $2.00 (re-fundable). Brochure - free. Satisfaction guaranteed.

Hewitt Research Foundation
established 1965
Director of Marketing
P.O. Box 9
2103 B Street
Washougal, WA 98671
Phone: 206-835-8708
Fax: 206-835-8697
Christian catalog

EDUCATIONAL RESOURCES Catalog, annual, ages 0-Adult. Focus: home schooling books and manipulatives. 10 day return policy. No restocking charge.

Holt Associates
established 1977
80% home schoolers
Patrick Farenga
Susannah Sheffer
2269 Massachusetts Ave.
Cambridge, MA 02140
Phone: 617-864-3100
E-mail: HOLT GWS.AOL
All-inclusive catalog

JOHN HOLT'S BOOK AND MUSIC STORE Catalog: 40,000+ circulation, contains literature selections, history, geography, audiocassettes, musical instruments, books on learning, etc. Books represent the philosophy of John Holt (children are natural learners, should be treated with many of the same rights as adults, and should be free to explore their world in their own way and at their own pace). Publishes Homeschooling List Packet of learning materials and resources, $4.00. Money back, credit, or exchange on any merchandise returned within 30 days of purchase.

Home and Hearth
established 1992
100% home schoolers
Lynn Knapik
Box 1176
Bow Island, AB T0K 0G0 Canada
Phone: 403-545-6021
Catalog

K-12, all educational products, supplementary science kits, games, parenting books. Canadian history and geography.

Home Learning Software
95% home schoolers
John Lind, Owner
PO Box 1948
Jamestown, NC 27282
Phone: 910-454-6361
Specialty catalog

HOME LEARNING SOFTWARE Catalog; 3x/year. Age group targeted: Two to adult. Focus: Educational computer shareware for IBM compatible computers.

Home on the Range
established 1993
99% home schoolers
Marcia Falleck
5912 - 24th Avenue South
Tampa, FL 33619
Phone: 813-622-8153
Fax: 813-622-8153
Christian catalog

Rubber stamps, stamp kits, art and craft supplies, foreign language, magnets and more.

Home School Books & Supplies
established 1985
80% home schoolers
Bill & Linda Jury
104 S. West Avenue
Arlington, WA 98223
Phone: 360-435-0376
Orders: 800-788-1221
Fax: 360-435-1028
Catalog and store
>   Over 450 publishers and over 100,000
>   titles available (stocking 20%). Currently
>   stocking educational software and CD
>   ROM titles. Catalog focus: curriculum,
>   supplemental education. Catalog is
>   released mid-April, no charge for catalog.

Home School Supply House
Brenda Frith
Box 5405
Drayton Valley, AB T7A 1R5 Canada
Phone: 403-696-2034
Christian catalog
>   Christian educational materials, with
>   some secular.

Homeschooler Helper
established 1992
100% home schoolers
Diane Dachyshyn
100A Ordze
Sherwood Park, AB T8B 1M6 Canada
Phone: 403-464-3066
Christian catalog and store
>   K-12, all subject areas.

Homeschooling Today
established 1992
98% home schoolers
Debbie Strayer, Editor
Route 2 Box 264
Hawthorne, FL 32640
Phone: 904-475-5869
Fax: 904-475-3088
E-mail: CompuServe 74672, 2004
Christian all-inclusive nonsectarian catalog
>   Home school and parent-involved educa-
>   tion. Preschool through high school.
>   100% satisfaction is guaranteed. To
>   receive a refund or exchange, the item
>   must be returned in its original, resalable
>   condition and within 45 days from
>   receipt. Exchanges must include ship-
>   ping charges just like a new order.

Homestead Learning
established 1993
100% home schoolers
Joan McKechnie
PO Box 275
Portland, PA 18351
Phone: 717-897-7774
Christian catalog
>   Parent helps, science, music, art, math,
>   language arts, social studies, and more,
>   K-12. Returns - 30 days with receipt.

Horn Book Inc.
established 1924
Eden Edwards, Marketing Manager
11 Beacon St., Ste. 1000
Boston, MA 02108
Phone: 617-227-1555 800-325-1170
Fax: 617-523-0299
Review Journal for Adults
>   Review journal of children's and young
>   adult books: THE HORN BOOK
>   MAGAZINE, reference guide to
>   children's and young adult books; THE
>   HORN BOOK GUIDE, and books about
>   children's literature.

Horne Book
established 1987
95% home schoolers
Earl & Phyllis Wiggins
953 Gardner Avenue
Ventura, CA 93004
Phone: 805-647-3907
Christian specialty catalog
History, reprints of old books. K-12 catalog.

ID-L Learning Resources
established 1993
95% home schoolers
Bev Cleveland
Box 399
Okotoks, AB T0L 1T0 Canada
Phone: 403-938-5042
All-inclusive catalog
K-12 catalog.

In One EAR Publications
established 1989
20% home schoolers
Elizabeth Reid, Marketing Director
29481 Manzanita Drive
Campo, CA 91906-1128
Phone: 619-478-5619
Fax: 619-478-5363
Catalog and store
Publish and sell educational materials especially related to "friendly foreign language learning." Quarterly catalog; age group targeted: K-adult. Focus: friendly foreign language learning. Free subscription to home school support groups. Satisfaction guaranteed or your money back - no questions asked.

Independent Institute
David Theroux, President
134 Ninety-Eighth Avenue
Oakland, CA 94603
Phone: 510-568-6047
Fax: 510-568-6040
Catalog
Philosophical focus: free markets, traditional values, individual rights, self-reliance and responsibility. Distributes semi-annual LIBERTY TREE: REVIEW AND CATALOG - featuring over 800 books, audiotapes, videos, games and collectibles for children ages 5+ through adults.

Informed Birth & Parenting
Rahima Baldwin
P.O. Box 3675
Ann Arbor, MI 48106
Phone: 313-662-6857
All-inclusive adult catalog
Informed Birth and Parenting Inquiries. Targets parents. Focus: alternatives in birth, Waldorf education, parenting.

Innovative & Quaint
established 1993
50% home schoolers
Lorraine C. Mabbett
Box 4873
West Hills, CA 91308
Phone: 818-884-4651
Fax: 818-884-1129
Catalog
Focus: Books; basic health & nutrition without New Age philosophies; literature, history, current political subjects; philosophy of business - healthy books! 1% per book, 20% maximum. Free freight.

Jewish Book Council
Carolyn Starman Hessel, Executive Director
15 East 26th Street
New York, NY 10010
Phone: 212-532-4949 X297
Fax: 212-481-4174
Jewish children and adult council
> The literary voice of the American Jewish community - sells bibliographies of related topics for all ages; JEWISH BOOK ANNUAL, JEWISH BOOK WORLD, issued 3 times yearly, and sponsor of National Jewish Book Awards.

Jonathan's Educational Resources
established 1987
30% home schoolers
Jonathan Katz
3100 N. Stone #116
Tucson, AZ 85705
Phone: 602-628-1108
Fax: 602-628-1188
All-inclusive catalog and store
> Primarily educational supply store that services the home school market. PreK-12, all educational subjects. 2nd store location: 7074 East Speedway, Tucson, AZ 85710, 602-885-9112.

Joshua's Christian Stores
Chris Laurie
3201 West Airport Freeway, Suite #102
Irving, TX 75062
Phone: 800-888-9641
Christian catalog and store for children and adults
> All Christian materials, gift items, mugs, frame prints, cards, books, cassettes, viedos, CDs, Bibles, T-shirts, and more.

Kids History Company
10% home schoolers
Jim Silverman
PO Box 1521
Sonoma, CA 95476
Phone: 707-996-0121
Fax: 707-938-8718
All-inclusive catalog
> Focus: children and U.S. history, grades 4-9.

KidsArt News
established 1986
Kim Solga
P.O. Box 274
309 Sheldon Ave.
Mt. Shasta,CA 96067
Phone: 916-926-5076   800-959-5076
Catalog
> Art supply catalog, including reviews for pre-K through high school. Selection of art activity books for ages preschool through high school - how to paint, how to draw, art teaching manuals, kits, videos and art supplies. No discount from regular catalog. Frequent sales offering discontinued or damaged items at substantial discounts. 100% satisfaction guaranteed or return of purchase price.

Kimbo Educational
established 1962
James Kimble
Amy Laufer
P.O. Box 477
10 N. Third Avenue
Long Branch, NJ 07740
Phone: 908-229-4949 (NJ) 800-631-2187
Fax: 908-870-3340
Specialty catalog
> Biannual catalog, mainly preK-3. Focus: educational cassettes, records, CD's, videos, etc.

Leafing Out
established 1991
80+% home schoolers
Jeff and Jackie Mattson, Director of Marketing
PO Box 220
Glen Ellyn, IL 60138-0220
Phone: 708-469-6109
Christian catalog
    K-12 educational materials plus parenting
    books.

Lifetime Canada
established 1994
90% home schoolers
Colin and Carol Singleton
4109 Pheasant Run
Mississauga, ON L5L 2C2 Canada
Phone: 905-828-1684
Christian all-inclusive catalog
    Lifetime Canada handles many of the
    same products as Lifetime in the U.S.,
    but with a Canadian emphasis. Lifetime
    Canada carries good books and educa-
    tional materials ranging from biographies
    to science for home and home education.
    Send $3.00 for 134-page annotated
    catalog.

Loompanics Unlimited
established 1975
Audrey Lee, General Manager
Box 1197
337 Sherman St.
Port Townsend, WA 98368
Phone: 360-385-5087
Fax: 360-385-7785
E-mail: loompanx@olympus.net
Adult catalog and book club
    Controversial and unusual books.
    Adults, over 18 years of age. Satisfaction
    guaranteed.

Making The Grade
established 1992
95% home schoolers
Mary E. Bachtel
c/o D.E.B.
844 Oak Road
Lakeville IN 46536
Phone: 219-784-3479
Christian all-inclusive catalog
    K-12, all educational materials. Nothing
    to conflict with Christian principles.

Master Desk Home School Supplies
99% home schoolers
Matt and Elaine Haynes
PO Box 152
Sexsmith, AB T0H 3C0 Canada
Phone: 403-568-2042
Christian catalog
    Biannual catalog. Focus: Christian home
    education and child training, family
    restoration.

Metamorphous Press, Inc.
established 1982
Maggie Connolly-Jensen
PO Box 10616
Portland, OR 97210
Phone: 503-228-4972
Metamorphous Press, Inc.—continued
Fax: 503-223-9117
Catalog
    Monthly catalog. Targets all ages. Self-
    help, books, tapes and videos.

More Than Books...
established 1992
100% home schoolers
Anne Cauley
Box 24145
300 Eagleson Road
Kanata, Ontario K2M 2C3 Canada
Phone: 613-592-4273
All-inclusive catalog
    K-12, all educational subjects.

Mustard Seed
established 1984
85% home schoolers
Molly Jacobsen
120 Winston Section Road
Winston, OR 97496
Phone: 503-679-3218
Christian all-inclusive catalog and store
    K-12, all educational subjects.

Nature Friend
established 1983
60-80% home schoolers
Stanley K. or Janice E. Brubaker
P.O. Box 73
Goshen, IN 46527
Phone: 219-534-2245
Fax: 219-534-2333
Christian specialty catalog
    PreK-12, science or nature oriented.

Our Father's House Press
established 1993
Margaret Dornay
5033 W. Mercer Way
Mercer Island,WA 98040
Phone: 206-232-7260
Fax: 206-232-2311
Catholic catalog
    OUR FATHER'S HOUSE CATHOLIC
    Catalog, with home schooling and after
    schooling articles and resources. Catho-
    lic World View-Classic form of educa-
    tion up to and including Renaissance.

Our Lady of the Rosary School
established 1983
100% home schoolers
Robert Brindle
105 E. Flaget Street
Bardstown, KY 40004
Phone: 502-348-1338
Fax: 502-348-1943

Catholic catalog
    Course catalog and has a small religious
    bookstore.

Parent's School Supply
established 1993
Mary Hennessey
5241 Springdale Rd.
Cincinnati, OH 45251
Phone: 513-741-3772
Fax: 513-741-9047
Catholic catalog
    Unit studies directed toward Catholics.
    All subjects, K-12. Catholic/Christian
    materials that don't conflict with Catholic
    philosophy.

Priority Book Service
established 1991
90% home schoolers
Sherry Woomert
HCR 62 Box 117
Moyie Springs, ID 83845
Phone: 208-267-3536
Christian all-inclusive book order service
    Book order service. General education
    for children through adults.

Quad Computing
Beverly Bafford
6744 Quad Lane
Eldersburg, MD 21784
Phone: 410-549-2223
All-inclusive catalog
    Catalog targets K-6th; all subject areas.

Quality Education Resources
established 1991
90% home schoolers
Carol & Gregg Mueller
P.O. Box 847, Cupertino, CA 95015-0847
Phone: 408-252-2254
Fax: 408-973-0470

Christian all-inclusive catalog
>   Focus: Products for teachers, home
>   educators, parents. K-12th grade. 30-day
>   return policy.

**Rainbow Connection and Compassion
Books**
established 1986
Donna O'Toole, Owner
477 Hannah Branch Road
Burnsville, NC 28714
Phone: 704-675-9670
Fax: 704-675-9687
Adult specialty catalog and book club
>   Books, audio, videos related to loss and
>   change of all kinds in peoples' lives,
>   including bereavement. All ages. We
>   offer bulk rates on 2 of our publications,
>   otherwise no discounts to the general
>   public.

Rennaissance Family Learning
established 1994
Cris Buckley
1301 South 35th Street
Omaha, NE 68105
Phone: 402-346-5148
Christian all-inclusive catalog
>   K-12 educational products; Greenleaf,
>   Five in a Row (literature based curricu-
>   lum for 4-8 years old). Focus: Unit
>   Studies.

Seton Home Study School
established 1981
Dr. Mary Kay Clark
1350 Progress Drive
Front Royal, VA 22630
Phone: 703-636-9990
Fax: 703-636-1602
Catholic catalog
>   K-12 Catholic correspondence.

Sing 'n Learn
established 1991
80% home schoolers
Sarah Cooper
2626 Club Meadow
Garland, TX 75043
Phone: 214-840-8342
Fax: 214-840-3187
Christian specialty catalog
>   K-12 products that use the medium of
>   music to teach all subjects, for example,
>   reading, math, etc.

Smart Stuff & Good Ideas
established 1992
48% home schoolers
Steve Bull
44-147 Bayview Haven
Kaneohe, HI 96744
Phone: 800-207-6278   808-247-3358
Fax: 808-247-3358
Specialty catalog
>   Catalog circulates 3x /year; 4yr.-adult.
>   Focus: Games for all children, especially
>   learning differenced and gifted.

Soft Winds Supply
established 1993
90% home schoolers
Edith Holenski
Box 40
Darlingford, MB R0G 0L0 Canada
Phone: 204-246-2083
Fax: 204-246-2190
Christian catalog and store
>   K-12, all educational subjects, Bible,
>   parent helps.

Steward Ship
established 1990
90% home schoolers
Jennifer and Jim Steward
PO Box 164
Garden Valley, CA 95633
Phone: 916-333-1642
Christian catalog
    Catalog focus: Unit study supplies.
    Philosophical focus: Whole learning life
    is school-real books-unit study/Christian.
    Grade levels: pre-K-8th; subject areas:
    unit study topical guides (Pilgrims,
    Columbus, Civil War, Medieval).

Sycamore Tree, Inc., The
established 1982
Sandy Gogel
2179 Meyer Place
Costa Mesa, CA 92627
Phone: 714-650-4466
Fax: 714-642-6750 or 800-779-6750 (orders)
Christian all-inclusive catalog
    Christian K-12, all educational subjects,
    with some secular. Has a baby/toddler
    section and lots of preschool items. 15
    day return for a full refund.

Trivium Pursuit
90% home schoolers
Laurie Bluedorn
139 Colorado, #168
Muscatine, IA 52761
Phone: 309-537-3641
Specialty catalog
    TRIVIUM PURSUIT Catalog, annual, all
    ages. Focus: Greek, Latin, logic, spelling.

Appendix

Book Resource Guides

AMERICAN LIBRARY ASSOC. BEST OF THE BEST FOR CHILDREN
Random House
Denise Perry Donavin, editor
ISBN 0-679-74250-6

AMERICAN LITERACY: Fifty Books that Define Our Culture and Ourselves
William Morrow
Jack Conway
ISBN 0-688-11963-8
The story behind 50 books and authors that influenced America: Thomas Paine's Common Sense, Martin Luther King's Letters from a Birmingham Jail, Frank Norris's The Octopus.

BABIES NEED BOOKS, out of print
Atheneum
Dorothy Butler
ISBN 0689111126
Early childhood (infants through six year-olds only), includes brief booklists at end of each chapter.

BEST BOOKS FOR KINDERGARTEN THROUGH HIGH SCHOOL
Bob Jones University Press
Christian
Annotated fiction titles, arranged by levels, including high school.

BIG BOOK OF HOME LEARNING, 4th edition
Crossway Books
Mary Pride
ISBN 0-89107-860-6
Fourth edition of this book to be released in Fall 1995 to include 750 reviews.

BOOK OF VIRTUES
Simon & Schuster
William Bennett
ISBN 0671683063
The book that was the catalyst for other character books recently published.

BOOKS CHILDREN LOVE
Crossway
Elizabeth Wilson
ISBN 0-89107-441-4
Lists hundreds of books from more than two dozen subject areas, with comments on each one: animals, art and architecture, Bible/spiritual teaching, biography, crafts and hobbies, dance, drama, geography, history, handicaps, horticulture, humor, language, literature, mathematics, music science, and others. Arranged by subject with recommended grade levels. Only books that hold children's attention, that are finely written and reflect basic Judeo-Christian values have been included.

BOOKS THAT BUILD CHARACTER:
A Guide to Teaching Your Child Moral
Values Through Stories
Simon & Schuster
William Kirkpatrick
ISBN 0-671-88423-9
Evaluations of more than 300 books that build a child's character. Divided into categories from fables and fairy tales through historical and contemporary fiction, history and biography to sacred text and more. Contains helpful chapter on "Selecting and Sharing Good Books: Some Guidelines."

CHRISTIAN HOME EDUCATORS'
CURRICULUM MANUAL - 2 volumes
Home Run Enterprises
Cathy Duffy
16172 Huxley Circle
Westminster, CA 92683
ISBN 0-929320-05-0
Phone: 714-841-1220
Thousands of educational products and resources reviewed in two volumes, an Elementary Edition and a Junior/Senior High School edition. Both revised for 1995. Elementary edition, 1995 now available. Jr./Sr. edition to be released soon. Query for availability.

CHOOSING BOOKS FOR CHILDREN:
A Commonsense Guide
Bantam Doubleday Dell
Betsy Hearne
ISBN 0-385-30108-1
How to choose appropriate books for children at different stages of development from preK through young adult fiction. More than 300 annotated selections.

CLASSICS TO READ ALOUD TO
YOUR CHILDREN
Crown
William F. Russell
ISBN 0-517-58715-7
See also by the same author: MORE CLASSICS TO READ ALOUD TO YOUR CHILDREN (ISBN 0-517-56108-5)

CLASSIC MYTHS TO READ ALOUD:
The Great Stories of Greek and Roman Mythology
Crown
William F. Russell
ISBN 0-517-58837-4
Specially arranged for Children five and up.

COMICS TO CLASSICS: A Parent's
Guide to Books for Teens and Preteens
Penguin
Arthea Reed
ISBN 0140237127
Directed at parents and teachers to help them encourage reading in teens. It features more than 300 titles for young people between the ages of 10 and 20. Books are categorized by themes and each listing includes a brief summary and age range.

EARLY SCHOOL YEARS READ
ALOUD PROGRAM
ETC Publications
Robert J. Whitehead
ISBN 0882800132
Four book set, one for each of the seasons, includes fiction and nonfiction titles for ages 4-8. Suggested read aloud titles are annotated with comprehension questions.

EYE OPENERS!
Viking
Beverly Kobrin
ISBN 0140468307
Over 500 books reviewed and listed by category, preK through Middle School nonfiction, incudes suggestions for organizing a reading room and a section for parents.

EYE OPENERS 2
Scholastic
Beverly Kobrin
ISBN 0590484028
Over 850 books reviewed and listed by category, preK through Middle School nonfiction.

FAMILY PROGRAM FOR READING ALOUD
Foundation for American Christian Education
Rosalie June Slater
PO Box 9444
Chesapeake, VA 23321-9444
Phone: 804-488-6601
FAX: 804-488-5593
ISBN 0-912498-09-9
Christian
Recommends books with values acceptable to the Christian family.

GOOD STUFF: Learning Tools for All Ages
Home Education Press
Becky Rupp
P.O. Box 1083
Tonasket, WA 98855
Phone: 509-486-1351
ISBN ISBN 0-945097-20-4
Hundreds of recommendations for books, magazines, catalogs, audio and video programs, equipment, games, educational toys, music resources, and more.

FOR READING OUT LOUD! A Guide to Sharing Books with Children
Bantam Doubleday Dell
Margaret Mary Kimmel and Elizabeth Segel
ISBN 0440504007
Targets books for elementary and middle school children. Recommends 140 books for read aloud, with annotations.

HOME SCHOOL MANUAL
Gazelle Publications
Ted Wade
1906 Niles-Buchanan Road
Niles, MI 49120
Phone: 616-465-4004
FAX: 616-465-4004
Lists curriculum reviews, as well as home school organizations in its appendix.

HOME SCHOOL SOURCE BOOK
Brook Farm Books
Don Reed
PO Box 246
Bridgewater, ME 04735
Reviews hundreds of home school resources.

HONEY FOR A CHILD'S HEART
Zondervan, distributed by HarperCollins
Gladys Hunt
ISBN 0310263816
Recommends books with good family values from a Christian perspective.

INTERNATIONAL READING ASSOCIATION
800 Barksdale Rd.
Newark, DE 19714
For parents: small publications available to help parents introduce books and reading to their children. Query for more information.

LET THE AUTHORS SPEAK
Old Pinnacle Publishing
Carolyn Hatcher
1048 Old Pinnacle Rd.
Joelton, TN 37080
Phone: 615-746-3342
Books are listed by historical setting (location and time period) then by author. Classics of world history, ancient through 19th century titles, primarily.

MARVA COLLINS' WAY
Jeremy P. Tarcher
Marva Collins and Civia Tamarkin
ISBN 0-87477-572-8
Contains a recommended reading and phonics list in the Appendix of this book.

NEW READ ALOUD HANDBOOK
Penguin
Jim Trelease
ISBN 0140468811
Read aloud favorites reviewed by book enthusiast Jim Trelease.

NEW YORK TIMES PARENT'S GUIDE TO THE BEST BOOKS FOR CHILDREN-revised and updated
Random House
Eden Ross Lipson
ISBN 0-812-91889-4
Over 3000 listings divided into: wordless, picture, story, early reading, mid level, and young adult. Includes author and illustrator index, cross-reference index by subjects.

NEWBERY AND CALDECOTT AWARDS: A Guide to the Medal and Honor Books
American Library Assoc.
50 E. Huron St.
Chicago, IL 60611
Phone: 1-800-545-2433
All winning titles since the inception of the awards are annotated in this book.

PARENT'S GUIDE TO CHILDREN'S READING: A Parent's Guide for Parents and Teachers of Boys and Girls under Thirteen
Nancy Larrick
out of print

PARENTS WHO LOVE READING, KIDS WHO DON'T: How it Happens and What You Can Do About It
Crown
Mary Leonhardt
ISBN 0-517-88222-1
How to turn your child into an avid reader even if he or she dislikes books.   Here's a teacher that believes most kids are pushed into learning disabilities classes unnecessarily.

READ FOR YOUR LIFE: Turning Teens into Readers
Zondervan, distributed by HarperCollins
Gladys Hunt
ISBN 0310548713
Annotated listings of books for teens, and how to critically read a book.

READING BETWEEN THE LINES: A Christian Guide to Literature
Crossway Books
Gene Edward Veith, Jr.
ISBN 089107-582-8

Book Guides and Resources from R. R. Bowker

PO Box 31
New Providence, NJ 07974
Phone: 908-464-6800   800-521-8110
Specializes in book guides and reference works
The following are especially helpful for use with young people.

A TO ZOO
Carolyn W. Lima and John A. Lima
ISBN 0-8352-3201-8
Guide to children's picture books, more than
14,000 fiction and nonfiction titles for preK
through second grade.

BEST BOOKS FOR CHILDREN™:
Preschool Through the Middle Grades
John T. Gillespie and Christine B. Gilbert
ISBN 0-8352-2131-8
Lists more than 11,000 titles that have
received three or more recommendations
from leading media reviews, arranged under
500 subject headings.

BEST BOOKS FOR JUNIOR HIGH
READERS™
John T. Gillespie
ISBN 0-8352-3020-1
Lists more than 11,000 titles that have
received three or more recommendations
from leading media reviews, arranged under
500 subject headings.

BEST BOOKS FOR SENIOR HIGH
READERS™
John T. Gillespie
ISBN 0-8352-3021-X
Lists more than 11,000 titles that have
received three or more recommendations
from leading media reviews, arranged under
500 subject headings.

BEYOND PICTURE BOOKS™
Barbara Barstow and Judith Riggle
ISBN 0-8352-2515-1
For work with ages 4-7. Includes 1600 titles.

BOOKS FOR THE GIFTED CHILD™
Barbara H. Baskin and Karen H. Harris
ISBN 0-8352-2131-8
150 annotated listings of contemporary
fiction and nonfiction titles.

BOOKS KIDS WILL SIT STILL FOR™
Judy Freeman
ISBN 0-8352-3010-4
Fiction, nonfiction, poetry, folklore, for PreK
through sixth grade, over 2100 recommended
titles.

FANTASY LITERATURE FOR CHILDREN & YOUNG ADULTS™
Ruth Nadelman Lynn
ISBN 0-8352-2347-7
Recommends over 3100 English and American fantasy novels and collections, indexed under 11 topics from Allegory and Fable to Witchcraft and Wizardry.

HIGH/LOW HANDBOOKS™: Books, Materials, and Services for the Problem Reader
Ellen V. LiBretto
ISBN 0-8352-2133-4
Includes 286 annotated entries, both fiction and nonfiction titles, including reading level and interest grade level.

JUNIORPLOTS 3™: A BOOK TALK GUIDE FOR USE WITH READERS AGES 12-16
ISBN 0-8352-2367-1
Eighty contemporary fiction and nonfiction titles arranged by genre.

PRIMARYPLOTS™: A Book Talk Guide for Readers Ages 5-8
Rebecca Thomas
ISBN 0-8352-2514-3
Includes 175 recommended, recently published titles grouped under themes for children: Respect for Nature & Living Things, Getting Along with Others, etc. Annotates each entry, includes reading level.

SENIORPLOTS™: A Book Talk Guide for Use with Readers Ages 15-18
John T. Gillespie and Corrine J. Naden
ISBN 0-8352-2513-5
Concise summaries of 80 works of contemporary fiction and nonfiction, grouped under: Growing Up to True Adventure and more.

YOUNG READER'S COMPANION™
Gorton Carruth
ISBN 0-8352-2765-0
Helps children and adults understand characters, plots and allusions in the books they read. Contains more than 2000 entries.

additional Bowker titles to consider

ACCEPT ME AS I AM: Best Books of Juvenile Nonfiction on Impairments and disabilities
AFRICAN BOOKS IN PRINT
BOOKS IN PRINT
BOOKS FOR THE GIFTED CHILD
BOOKS TO HELP CHILDREN COPE WITH SEPARATION AND LOSS
BOOKS OUT-OF-PRINT
CHALLENGING THE GIFTED
CHILDREN'S BOOKS IN PRINT
EL-HI TEXTBOOKS AND SERIALS IN PRINT
FICTION, FOLKLORE, FANTASY AND POETRY FOR CHILDREN 1876-1985
GLOBAL VOICES, GLOBAL VISIONS: A Core Collection of Multicultural Books
INTERNATIONAL PERIODICALS DIRECTORY
INDEX TO COLLECTIVE BIOGRAPHIES FOR YOUNG READERS: Elementary and Junior High Level.
LITERARY MARKET PLACE
MORE NOTES FROM A DIFFERENT DRUMMER: A Guide to Juvenile Fiction Portraying the Disabled
NOTES FROM A DIFFERENT DRUMMER: A Guide to Juvenile Fiction Portraying the Handicapped
REFERENCE BOOKS FOR YOUNG READERS
RELIGIOUS AND INSPIRATIONAL BOOKS AND SERIALS IN PRINT
SUBJECT GUIDE TO CHILDREN'S BOOKS IN PRINT
VARIETY'S COMPLETE HOME VIDEO DIRECTORY

Many more titles are available. Secure a copy of their catalog.

Magazines and Newsletters
that review Children's Books, Audio, etc.

BOOK LINKS
American Library Assoc.
50 E. Huron Street
Chicago, IL 60611-9969
Phone: 312-944-6780; 800-545-2433
FAX: 312-337-6787
Magazine that is theme oriented. Great for unit study or for integrating subjects.

BULLETIN OF THE CENTER FOR CHILDREN'S BOOKS
University of Chicago
1512 N. Fremont
Chicago, IL 60622
Phone: 312-944-5253

HORN BOOK MAGAZINE
HORN BOOK GUIDE
Horn Book Inc.
Eden Edwards, Marketing Manager
11 Beacon St., Ste. 1000
Boston, MA 02108
Phone: 617-227-1555   800-325-1170
FAX: 617-523-0299
Review journal of children's and young adult books: THE HORN BOOK MAGAZINE, reference guide to children's and young adult books; THE HORN BOOK GUIDE, and books about children's literature.

IN REVIEW: Living Books Past and Present
Bethlehem Books
RR 1 Box 137A
Minto, ND 58261

Phone: 701-248-3866
Published quarterly to promote interest in and provide information about wholesome children's books written from the early 1900's through the 1970's.

KLIATT
33 Bay Street Road.
Wellesley, MA 02181
Phone: 617-237-7577
Review children's paperbacks.

KOBRIN LETTER
Beverly Kobrin
732 Greer Rd.
Palo Alto, CA 94303
Phone: 415-856-6658
Review letter published 6x per year. Review children's nonfiction, preK through Middle School, all subjects.

PARENTS' CHOICE
Parents' Choice Foundation
Box 185
Waban, MA 02168
Review publication for children's books, movies, audio, toys and more.

SCHOOL LIBRARY JOURNAL
249 W. 17th St.
New York, NY 10011
Phone: 212-463-6759
FAX: 212-463-6689
More than 2800 reviews of educational materials annually. Eleven issues per year.

Home School Favorites

(If you want help selecting resources for your home schooled children,
these guides have stood the test of time.)

BEST BOOKS FOR KINDERGARTEN THROUGH HIGH SCHOOL
Bob Jones University Press
Greenville, SC 29614
800-845-5731
Christian
Annotated fiction titles, arranged by levels, including high school.

BIG BOOK OF HOME LEARNING, 4th edition
Crossway Books
Mary Pride
ISBN 0-89107-860-6
Christian
Fourth edition of this book to be released in Fall 1995 to include 750 reviews.

BOOKS CHILDREN LOVE
Crossway
Elizabeth Wilson
ISBN 0-89107-441-4
Christian
Lists hundreds of books from more than two dozen subject areas, with comments on each one: animals, art and architecture, Bible/ spiritual teaching, biography, crafts and hobbies, dance, drama, geography, history, handicaps, horticulture, humor, language, literature, mathematics, music science, and others. Arranged by subject with recommended grade levels. Only books that hold children's attention, that are finely written and reflect basic Judeo-Christian values have been included.

CHRISTIAN HOME EDUCATORS' CURRICULUM MANUAL - 2 volumes
Home Run Enterprises
Cathy Duffy
16172 Huxley Circle
Westminster, CA 92683
ISBN 0-929320-05-0
Phone: 714-841-1220
Christian
Thousands of educational products and resources reviewed in two volumes, an Elementary Edition and a Junior/Senior High School edition. Both revised for 1995. Elementary edition, 1995 now available. Jr./ Sr. edition to be released soon. Query for availability.

FAMILY PROGRAM FOR READING ALOUD
Foundation for American Christian Education
Rosalie June Slater
PO Box 9444
Chesapeake, VA 23321-9444
Phone: 804-488-6601
FAX: 804-488-5593
ISBN 0-912498-09-9
Christian
Recommends books with values acceptable to the Christian family.

GOOD STUFF: Learning Tools for All Ages
Home Education Press
Becky Rupp
P.O. Box 1083
Tonasket, WA 98855
Phone: 509-486-1351
ISBN ISBN 0-945097-20-4
All inclusive
Hundreds of recommendations for books, magazines, catalogs, audio and video programs, equipment, games, educational toys, music resources, and more.

HOME SCHOOL MANUAL
Gazelle Publications
Ted Wade
1906 Niles-Buchanan Road
Niles, MI 49120
Phone: 616-465-4004
FAX: 616-465-4004
Christian
Lists curriculum reviews, as well as home school organizations in its appendix.

HOME SCHOOL SOURCE BOOK
Brook Farm Books
Don Reed
PO Box 246
Bridgewater, ME 04735

HONEY FOR A CHILD'S HEART
Zondervan, distributed by HarperCollins
Gladys Hunt
ISBN 0310263816
Recommends books with good family values from a Christian perspective.

LET THE AUTHORS SPEAK
Old Pinnacle Publishing
Carolyn Hatcher
1048 Old Pinnacle Rd.
Joelton, TN 37080
Phone: 615-746-3342

Books are listed by historical setting (location and time period) then by author. Classics of world history, ancient through 19th century titles, primarily.

READ FOR YOUR LIFE: Turning Teens into Readers
Zondervan, distributed by HarperCollins
Gladys Hunt
ISBN 0310548713
Annotated listings of books for teens, and how to critically read a book.

READING BETWEEN THE LINES: A Christian Guide to Literature
Crossway Books
Gene Edward Veith, Jr.
ISBN 089107-582-8

National Home School Organizations

(contact these organizations for curriculum fair information in your area)

National Center for Home Education
PO Box 125
Paeonian Springs, VA 22129
Phone: 703-338-7600
FAX: 703-338-9333
Christian national home school organization.

National Homeschool Association
PO Box 157290
Cincinnati, OH 45215-7290
Phone: 513-772-9580
National home school organization, all-inclusive.

Books that List Cost-Saving Ideas, Where to Buy Free, or at Discount

ELEMENTARY TEACHERS GUIDE TO FREE CURRICULUM MATERIALS
Educators Progress Service
Thomas J. Haider, editor
214 Center St.
Randolph, WI 53956-1497
Phone: 414-326-3126
FAX: 414-326-3127

FREE AND ALMOST FREE THINGS FOR TEACHERS
Putnam Publishing
Susan Osborn
ISBN 0-399-51795-2
More than 250 educational resources-yours for the asking or at a cost of $5 or less.

FREE STUFF FOR KIDS
Meadowbrook Press
ISBN 0-88166-212-7
Hundreds of free and up-to-a-dollar things kids can send for by mail!

MISERLY MOMS: Living on One Income in a Two Income Economy
Miserly Moms
Jonni Stivers McCoy
PO Box 32174
San Jose, CA 95152-2174

NEVER THROW OUT A BANANA AGAIN and 364 other ways to save money at home (without knocking yourself out)
Crown
Martha M. Bullen and Darcie Sanders
ISBN 0-517-884208
Tofu, car dealers, car maintenance, plant perennials and self-sowing annuals, insulate with ivy, install an attic fan, say good-bye to annual fees on credit cards and more ideas.

SAVE YOUR BUSINESS A BUNDLE: 202 Ways to Cut Costs and Boost Profits Now—For Companies of Any Size
Simon & Schuster
Daniel Kehrer
ISBN 0-671-78893-0
Includes: how to banish service contracts; slashing overseas mailing costs; how to negotiate lower hotel, airline and car rental rates, and more. Includes names, addresses, price and telephone numbers for cost cutting.

SAVING ON A SHOESTRING: How to Cut Expenses, Reduce Debt , Stash More Cash
Dearborn Publishing
Barbara O'Neill
ISBN 0-7931-1118-8
Financial planning ideas for everyone.
Includes: 25 ways to save money, 50 ways to cut expenses, 15 ways to reduce debt.

SMALL BUSINESS; BIG SAVINGS: Where and How to Save Money on Everything Your Business Needs
HarperReference
Laura Teller and Warren R. Schatz
ISBN 0-06-273298-6
Directory of discount and wholesale sources of business supplies, equipment and services. Organized by expense category and lists names, addresses, product line descriptions, telephone and fax numbers.

TIGHTWAD GAZETTE II: Promoting Thrift as a Viable Alternative Lifestyle
Random House
Amy Dacyczyyn
ISBN 0-679-75078-9
This new book gives information on secondary uses for junk mail, old blue jeans; when to use coupons; how to negotiate; lessons from the Great Depression; how to cut your food bill in half. Also see her first book: THE TIGHTWAD GAZETTE, 0-679-74388-X.

WHERE TO SELL IT DIRECTORY
Pilot Books
103 Cooper Street
Babylon, NY 11702
1995 edition sells for $5.95, plus $1.00 shipping and handling. Prefer orders come via mail.

WHOLESALE- BY- MAIL CATALOG 1995: How Consumers Can Shop by Mail, Phone, or Online Service and Save 30% to 90% off List Price
HarperReference
Lowell Miller and Prudence McCullough
ISBN 0-06-273310-9
Includes more than 500 companies with products from: computers, consumer electronics, appliances, designer fashions, toys, tools, crafts, jewelry, beauty products, and more. Special reader-only discounts are included throughout the book. Indexed by both products and company name.

Books and Resources Recommended by Jane A. Williams

ARE YOU LIBERAL? CONSERVATIVE? OR CONFUSED?
Bluestocking Press
ISBN 0-942617-23-1
PO Box 1014
Placerville, CA 95667
Phone: 800-959-8586; 916-621-1123
FAX: 916-642-9222
Author Richard Maybury gives an excellent explanation of why history books are slanted, and why the predominant viewpoint reported are liberal and conservative, to the exclusion of most others.

BASIC COLLEGE MATHEMATICS, 4th edition
HarperCollins Publishers
Miller, Salzman and Hestwood
10 East 53rd St.
New York, NY 10022

BOOKS AND LIBRARIES
HarperTrophy
Jack Knowlton
ISBN 0-06-446153-X
Picture book for ages 7-10 shows the evolution of books and the creation of the first libraries — including a depiction of the Dewey Decimal System.

ECONOMICS IN ONE LESSON
Crown Trade Paperbacks, NY
Henry Hazlitt
ISBN 0-517-54823-2

ELEMENTS OF...
Macmillan Publishing Co.
MacMillan-Indianapolis, Indiana
Phone: 800-223-2336
Includes ELEMENTS OF GRAMMAR; ELEMENTS OF EDITING; ELEMENTS OF STYLE.

FRANKLIN LEARNING RESOURCES
122 Burrs Rd.
Mt. Holly, NJ 08060
Phone: 800-525-9673
Fax: 609-261-8368
Manufacturers the Franklin Digital Book® System: includes Merriam-Wesbster® Dictionary, Concise Columbia Encyclopedia, and more.

HOW TO LIE WITH STATISTICS
W.W. Norton
Darrell Huff
ISBN 0-393310728

THE LAW
Frederic Bastiat
Foundation for Economic Education
Irvington-on-Hudson, NY

TIMETABLES OF HISTORY™
ISBN 0-671-74271-X
Simon & Schuster
1230 Avenue of the Americas
New York, NY 10020
Phone: 800-223-2336

UNCLE ERIC'S MODEL OF HOW THE WORLD WORKS
Bluestocking Press
PO Box 1014
Placerville, CA 95667
Phone: 800-959-8586; 916-621-1123
FAX: 916-642-9222
Six books written by Richard J. Maybury that give children and adults the tools they need to understand how the world works. Philosophy represented by Mr. Maybury is consistent with that of America's Founders. Books in this series are:

UNCLE ERIC TALKS ABOUT PERSONAL, CAREER
    AND FINANCIAL SECURITY
WHATEVER HAPPENED TO PENNY CANDY?
WHATEVER HAPPENED TO JUSTICE?
ARE YOU LIBERAL? CONSERVATIVE? OR
    CONFUSED?
ANCIENT ROME: HOW IT AFFECTS YOU TODAY
EVALUATING BOOKS: WHAT WOULD THOMAS
    JEFFERSON THINK ABOUT THIS?

WEBSTER'S 1828 DICTIONARY
Foundation for American Christian Education
PO Box 9444
Chesapeake, VA 23321-9444
Phone: 804-488-6601
FAX: 804-488-5593
Reprint of the original 1828 dictionary.
Good book for comparing the differences in the evolving definitions of language from America's founding to today.

WORLD PRESS REVIEW
200 Madison Ave.
New York, NY 10016
Phone: 212-889-5155
FAX: 212-889-5634
Monthly magazine. Annual subscription price as of April 1995: $24.97. Confirm price before ordering. Each article provides the following information: Date article first appeared, source of the article, name of the writer, and writer's political affiliation.

On-Line Resources

GUIDE TO INFORMATION ACCESS: A Complete Research Handbook and Directory
Random House
Sandy Whiteley, Editor
ISBN 0-679-75075-4
Includes the Internet and Other Electronic Sources. Selects more than 3000 of the best standard and electronic sources in the 36 most-researched subject categories, tell where to find them, and explains the latest research. Prepared under the auspices of the American Library Association.

KIDS ON LINE: 150 Ways for Kids to Surf the Net for Fun and Information
Avon
Marian Salzman and Robert Pondiscio
ISBN 0-380-78231-6
Describes what's available to kids on all the on-line programs. Features comprehensive information about Internet, CompuServe and Prodigy. Tells young readers what's free and what's not, cost breakdown, and how to get on-line.

Index

Bluestocking Press